APPARITIONS;

OR,

THE MYSTERY OF
GHOSTS, HOBGOBLINS,
AND
HAUNTED HOUSES,
DEVELOPED.

"Animum rege."

** "This Collection of Stories is well chosen, and affords a fund of amusement that is cheap at the price of five shillings. By putting such a book as this into the hands of children, parents will more effectually guard their minds against weak credulity, than by grave philosophic admonition."

Monthly Review, October 1814.

British Library Cataloguing-in-Publication Data
A catalogue record for this book is available from
the British Library

H Corbould delin.ᵗ C Knight sculp.ᵗ 1814

The Haunted Beach.

CONTENTS

APPARITIONS;
OR,
THE MYSTERY OF GHOSTS, HOBGOBLINS, AND HAUNTED HOUSES, *DEVELOPED.*

BEING A COLLECTION OF
ENTERTAINING STORIES,
FOUNDED ON FACT,
And selected for the purpose of
ERADICATING THOSE FEARS,
WHICH THE IGNORANT, THE WEAK,
AND THE SUPERSTITIOUS,
ARE BUT TOO APT TO ENCOURAGE,
FOR WANT OF PROPERLY EXAMINING INTO THE
CAUSES OF SUCH ABSURD IMPOSITIONS.

BY JOSEPH TAYLOR.

INTRODUCTION.

The subsequent little Work owes its rise and progress to very trifling circumstances.

In the early part of my life, having read many books in favour of Ghosts and Spectral Appearances, the recollection remained so strong in my mind, that, for *years* after, the dread of phantoms bore irresistible sway. This dread continued till about my twenty-third year, when the following simple affair fully convinced me, how necessary it was *thoroughly* to investigate *every thing* that tended to supernatural agency, lest idle fear should gain a total ascendancy over my mind.

About this period, I had apartments in a large old-fashioned country mansion. From my bed-chamber was a secret door leading to a private staircase, which communicated with some of the lower rooms. This door was fastened both within and without; consequently all fear of intrusion from that quarter was entirely removed. However, at times, I could not help ruminating on the malpractices that *might* have been committed by evil-disposed persons, through this communication; and "busy meddling fancy" was fertile in conjuring up imaginary horrors. Every thing, however, was quiet, and agreeable to my wishes, for some months after my arrival. One moonlight night, in the month of June, I retired to my bed, full of thought, but slept soundly till about one o'clock; when I awoke, and discovered, by the help of the moon which shone full in my room, a tall figure in white, with arms extended, at the foot of my bed. Fear and astonishment overpowered me for a few seconds; I gazed on it with terror, and was afraid to move. At length I had courage to take a *second* peep at this disturber of my rest, and still continued much alarmed, and irresolute how to act. I hesitated whether to speak to the figure, or arouse the family. The first idea I considered as a dangerous act of heroism; the latter, as a risk of being laughed at, should the subject of my story not prove supernatural. Therefore, after taking a *third* view of the phantom, I mustered up all my resolution, jumped out of bed, and boldly went up to the figure, grasped it round and round, and found it incorporeal. I then looked at it again, and felt it again; when, reader, judge of my astonishment—this ghostly spectre proved to be nothing more than a large new flannel dressing-gown which had been sent home to me in the course of the day, and which had been hung on some pegs against the wainscot at the foot of my bed. One arm accidentally crossed two or three of the adjoining pegs, and the other was nearly parallel by coming in contact with some article of furniture which stood near. Now the mystery was developed: this dreadful hobgoblin, which a few minutes before I began to think was an aërial being, or sprite, and which must have gained admission either through the key-hole, or under the door, turned out to be my own garment. I smiled at my groundless fears, was pleased with any resolution, returned light-hearted to my bed, and moralized nearly the whole of the night on the simplicity of a great part of mankind in being so credulous as to believe every idle tale, or conceive every noise to be a spectre, without first duly examining into causes.

This very trifling accident was of great service to me

as I travelled onward through life. Similar circumstances transpired. Screams, and shades, I encountered; which always, upon due investigation, ended in "trifles light as air."

Nor did the good end here. My story circulated, and put other young men upon the alert, to guard against similar delusions. They likewise imparted to me their ghostly encounters, and those I thought deserving of record I always committed to writing; and, as many of them are well authenticated facts, and both instructive and amusing, they form a part of the volume now presented to the Public.

The other stories are selected from history, and respectable publications; forming in the whole, I hope, an antidote against a too credulous belief in every village tale, or old gossip's story.

Though I candidly acknowledge to have received great pleasure in forming this Collection, I would by no means wish it to be imagined, that I am sceptical in my opinions, or entirely disbelieve and set my face against all apparitional record. No; I do believe that, for certain purposes, and on certain and all-wise occasions, such things *are*, and *have been* permitted by the Almighty; but by no means do I believe they are suffered to appear half so frequently as our modern ghost-mongers manufacture them. Among the various idle tales in circulation, nothing is more common than the prevalent opinion concerning what is generally called a *death-watch*, and which is vulgarly believed to foretel the death of some one in the family. "This is, " observes a writer in the Philosophical Transactions, "a ridiculous fancy crept into vulgar heads, and employed to terrify and affright weak people as a monitor of approaching death." Therefore, to prevent such causeless fears, I shall take this opportunity to undeceive the world, by shewing what it is, and that no such thing is intended by it. It has obtained the name of death-watch, by making a little clinking noise like a watch; which having given some disturbance to a gentleman in his chamber, who was not to be affrighted with such vulgar errors, it tempted him to a diligent search after the true cause of this noise, which I shall relate in his own words.

"I have been, some time since, accompanied with this little noise. One evening, I sat down by a table from whence the noise proceeded, and laid my watch upon the same, and perceived, to my admiration, that the sound made by this invisible automaton was louder than that of the artificial machine. Its vibrations would fall as regular, but much quicker. Upon a strict examination, it was found to be nothing but a little beetle, or spider, in the wood of a box." Sometimes they are found in the plastering of a wall, and at other times in a rotten post, or in some old chest or trunk; and the noise is made by beating its head on the subject that it finds fit for sound. "The little animal that I found, " says the gentleman, "was about two lines and a half long, calling a line the eighth part of an inch. The colour was a dark brown, with spots somewhat lighter, and irregularly placed, which could not easily be rubbed off." It was sent to the publisher of the Philosophical Transactions of the Royal Society.

Some people, influenced by common report, have fancied this little animal a spirit sent to admonish them of their deaths; and, to uphold the fancy, tell you of other strange monitors altogether as ridiculous. Though, as I before observed, I do not deny but the Almighty may employ unusual methods to warn us at times of our approaching ends, yet in general, such common and unaccountable tales are mere nonsense, originating from want of a proper investigation, and kept alive by an infatuated delight in telling strange stories, rendered more ridiculous by recapitulation. How charmingly does our poet Thomson touch upon this subject—

"Meantime the village rouses up the fire;
While, well attested, and as well believ'd,
Heard solemn, goes the goblin story round;
Till superstitious horror creeps o'er all."

How cautious then ought parents and guardians to be over their children, and the young people committed to their charge. For, says an elegant writer, the superstitious impressions made upon their minds, by the tales of weak and ignorant people in their infancy; a time when the tender mind is most apt to receive the impressions of error and vice, as well as those of truth and virtue, and, having once received either the one or the other, is likely to retain them as long as it subsists in the body. All these deplorable follies proceed from wrong and unworthy apprehensions of God's providence, in his care of man, and government of the world. Surely no reasonable creature can ever imagine, that the all-wise God should inspire owls and ravens to hoot out the elegies of dying men; that he should have ordained a fatality in numbers, inflict punishment without an offence; and that being one amongst the fatal number at a table, should be a crime (though contrary to no command) not to be expiated but by death! Thus folly, like gunpowder, runs in a train from one generation to another, preserved and conveyed by the perpetual tradition of tattling gossips.

I now conclude this Introduction; and, in the following pages, shall present my readers with some admirable Essays on the subject by eminent writers: and a Collection of Stories will follow, which, I trust, will not only entertain, but likewise convince the *thinking* part of mankind of the absurdity in believing every silly tale without first tracing the promulgation to its original source; for

"Whatever warms the heart, or fills the head,
As the mind opens, and its functions spread,
Imagination plies her dangerous art,
And pours it all upon the peccant part."

J. TAYLOR.
London, March 20, 1815.

AN ESSAY ON
GHOSTS AND APPARITIONS.

There is no folly more predominant, in the country at least, than a ridiculous and superstitious fear of ghosts and apparitions. Servants, nurses, old women, and others of the same standard of wisdom, to pass away the tediousness of a winter's evening, please and terrify themselves, and the children who compose their audience, with strange relations of these things, till they are even afraid of removing their eyes from one another, for fear of seeing a *pale spectre* entering the room. Frightful ideas raised in the minds of children take so strong a possession of the faculties, that they often remain for ever fixed, and all the arguments of reason are unable to remove them. Hence it is, that so many grown-up people still keep the ridiculous fears of their infancy. I know a lady, of very good sense in other things, who, if she is left by herself after ten o'clock at night, will faint away at the terror of thinking some horrid spectre, with eyes sunk, meagre countenance, and threatening aspect, is standing at her elbow. And an Officer in the Guards, of my acquaintance, who has often, abroad, shewn no concern in marching up to the mouth of a cannon, has not courage enough to be in the dark without company. As I take the fear of ghosts, like all other prejudices, to be imbibed in our infancy, I would recommend this advice to parents—to use the utmost care, that the minds of their children are not vitiated by their servants' tales of ghosts, hobgoblins, and bugbears; which, though told to please, or frighten them into good, seldom fail of producing the very worst effects.

There are some who are ghost-mad, and terrify themselves,

because the Scripture has mentioned the appearance of ghosts. I shall not dispute, but, by the power of God, an incorporeal being may be visible to human eyes; but then, an all-wise Power would not have recourse to a preternatural effect but on some important occasion. Therefore, my intention is only to laugh a ridiculous fear out of the world, by shewing on what absurd and improbable foundations the common nature of ghosts and apparitions are built.

In the country, there are generally allowed to be two sorts of ghosts;—the vulgar ghost, and the ghost of dignity. The latter is always the spirit of some Lord of the Manor, or Justice of the Peace, who, still desirous to see how affairs go on in his parish, rattles through it in a coach and six, much about midnight. This ghost is, in every respect, the very same man that the person whom he represents was in his life-time. Nay, the spirit, though incorporeal, has on its body all the marks which the Squire had on his; the scar on the cheek, the dimple on the chin, and twenty other demonstrative signs, which are visible to any old woman in the parish, that can *see clearly in a dark night!*

The ghost keeps up to the character of a good old grave gentleman, who is heartily sorry to think his son will not live upon his estate, but rambles up to London, and runs it out, perhaps, in extravagance. He therefore does nothing inconsistent with the gravity of his character; but, still retaining the generous heart of a true Briton, keeps up his equipage, and loves good living and hospitality; for, a little time after the coach and six has, with a solemn rumble, passed through the village into his own court-yard, there is a great noise heard in the house, of servants running up and down stairs, the jacks going, and a great clattering of plates and dishes. Thus he spends an hour or two every midnight, in living well, after he has been some years dead; but is complaisant enough to leave every thing, at his departure, in the same position that he found them.

There is scarcely a little town in all England, but has an old female spirit appertaining to it, who, in her high-crown hat, nicely clean linen, and red petticoat, has been viewed by half the parish. This article of dress is of mighty concern among some ghosts; wherefore a skilful and learned apparition writer, in the Preface of Drelincourt on Death, makes a very pious ghost talk to a lady upon the important subject of scouring a mantua. Before I leave my ghost of dignity, I must take notice of some who delight to seem as formidable as possible, and who are not content with appearing without heads themselves, but their coachmen and horses must be without their's too, and the coach itself frequently all on fire. These spirits, I know not for what reason, are universally allowed to have been people of first quality, and courtiers.

As for the vulgar ghost, it seldom appears in its own bodily likeness, unless it be with a throat cut from ear to ear, or a winding-sheet; but humbly contents itself with the body of a white horse, that gallops over the meadows without legs, and grazes without a head. On other occasions, it takes the appearance of a black shock dog, which, with great goggle, glaring eyes, stares you full in the face, but never hurts you more than unmannerly pushing you from the wall. Sometimes a friendly ghost surprises you with a hand as cold as clay; at other times, that same ghostly hand gives three solemn raps, with several particularities, according to the different dispositions of the ghost.

The chief reason which calls them back again to visit the world by night, is their fondness for some old broad pieces, or a pot of money, they buried in their life-time; and they cannot rest to have it lie useless, therefore the gold raises them before the resurrection.

Mr. Addison's charming Essay, in the *Spectator,* is so applicable and prefatory to a work of this nature, that we cannot resist inserting that inimitable production in his own words.

"Going to dine, " says he, "with an old acquaintance, I had the misfortune to find his whole family very much dejected.

Upon asking him the occasion of it, he told me that his wife had dreamt a strange dream the night before, which they were afraid portended some misfortune to themselves or to their children. At her coming into the room, I observed a settled melancholy in her countenance, which I should have been troubled for, had I not heard from whence it proceeded. We were no sooner sat down, but, after having looked upon me a little while, 'My dear, ' says she, turning to her husband, 'you may now see the stranger that was in the candle last night.' Soon after this, as they began to talk of family affairs, a little boy at the lower end of the table told her, that he was to go into join-hand on Thursday. 'Thursday!' says she; 'no, child; if it please God, you shall not begin upon Childermas-day; tell your writing-master, that Friday will be soon enough.' I was reflecting with myself on the oddness of her fancy, and wondering that any body would establish it as a rule to lose a day in every week. In the midst of these my musings, she desired me to reach her a little salt upon the point of my knife, which I did in such a trepidation and hurry of obedience, that I let it drop by the way; at which she immediately startled, and said it fell towards her. Upon this I looked very blank; and, observing the concern of the whole table, began to consider myself, with some confusion, as a person that had brought a disaster upon the family. The lady, however, recovering herself after a little space, said to her husband, with a sigh, 'My dear, misfortunes never come single.' My friend, I found, acted but an under part at his table; and, being a man of more good-nature than understanding, thinks himself obliged to fall in with all the passions and humours of his yoke-fellow. 'Do not you remember, child, ' said she, 'that the pigeon-house fell the very afternoon that our careless wench spilt the salt upon the table?' 'Yes, ' says he, 'my dear; and the next post brought us an account of the battle of Almanza.' The reader may guess at the figure I made, after having done all this mischief. I dispatched my dinner as soon as I could, with my usual taciturnity; when, to my utter confusion, the lady seeing me quitting my knife and fork, and laying them across one another upon the plate, desired me that I would humour her so far as to take them out of that figure, and place them side by side. What the absurdity was which I had committed, I did not know, but I suppose there was some traditionary superstition in it; and therefore, in obedience to the lady of the house, I disposed of my knife and fork in two parallel lines, which is the figure I shall always lay them in for the future, though I do not know any reason for it.

"It is not difficult for a man to see that a person has conceived an aversion to him. For my own part, I quickly found, by the lady's looks, that she regarded me as a very odd kind of fellow, with an unfortunate aspect. For which reason I took my leave immediately after dinner, and withdrew to my own lodgings. Upon my return home, I fell into a profound contemplation on the evils that attend these superstitious follies of mankind; how they subject us to imaginary afflictions and additional sorrows, that do not properly come within our lot. As if the natural calamities of life were not sufficient for it, we turn the most indifferent circumstances into misfortunes, and suffer as much from trifling accidents as from real evils. I have known the shooting of a star spoil a night's rest; and have seen a man in love grow pale, and lose his appetite, upon the plucking of a merry-thought. A screech-owl at midnight has alarmed a family more than a band of robbers; nay, the voice of a cricket hath struck more terror than the roaring of a lion. There is nothing so inconsiderable, which may not appear dreadful to an imagination that is filled with omens and prognostics. A rusty nail, or a crooked pin, shoot up into prodigies.

"I remember, I was once in a mixed assembly, that was full of noise and mirth, when on a sudden an old woman unluckily observed there were thirteen of us in company. This remark struck a panic terror into several who were present, insomuch that one or two of the ladies were going to leave the room: but a friend of mine, taking notice that one of our female companions was big with child, affirmed there were fourteen in the room; and that, instead of portending one of the company should die, it plainly foretold one of them should be born. Had not my friend found out this expedient to break the omen, I question not but half the women in the company would have fallen sick that very night.

"An old maid, that is troubled with the vapours, produces infinite disturbances of this kind among her friends and neighbours. I once knew a maiden aunt, of a great family, who is one of these antiquated sybils, that forebodes and prophesies from one end of the year to the other. She is always seeing apparitions, and hearing death-watches; and was the other day almost frightened out of her wits by the great house-dog, that howled in the stable at a time when she lay ill of the tooth-ach. Such an extravagant cast of mind engages multitudes of people not only in impertinent terrors, but in supernumerary duties of life; and arises from that fear and ignorance which are natural to the soul of man. The horror with which we entertain the thoughts of death or indeed of any future evil, and the uncertainty of its approach, fill a melancholy mind with innumerable apprehensions and suspicions, and consequently dispose it to the observation of such groundless prodigies and predictions. For, as it is the chief concern of wise men to retrench the evils of life by the reasonings of philosophy, it is the employment of fools to multiply them by the sentiments of superstition.

"For my own part, I should be very much troubled, were I endowed with this divining quality, though it should inform me truly of every thing that can befal me. I would not anticipate the relish of any happiness, nor feel the weight of any misery, before it actually arrives.

"I know but one way of fortifying my soul against these gloomy presages and terrors of mind; and that is, by securing to myself the friendship and protection of that Being who disposes of events, and governs futurity. He sees at one view the whole thread of my existence; not only that part of it which I have already passed through, but that which runs forward into all the depths of eternity. When I lay me down to sleep, I recommend myself to his care; when I awake, I give myself up to his direction. Amidst all the evils that threaten me, I will look up to him for help and question not but he will either avert them, or turn them to my advantage. Though I know neither the time nor the manner of the death I am to die, I am not at all solicitous about it; because I am sure that he knows them both, and that he will not fail to comfort and support me under them."

In another paper, the same gentleman thus expresses himself on the same subject:—

"I remember, last winter, there were several young girls of the neighbourhood sitting about the fire with my landlady's daughters, and telling stories of spirits and apparitions. Upon my opening the door, the young women broke off their discourse; but my landlady's daughters telling them it was nobody but the gentleman (for that is the name which I go by in the neighbourhood as well as in the family), they went on without minding me. I seated myself by the candle that stood on a table at one end of the room; and, pretending to read a book that I took out of my pocket, heard several dreadful stories of ghosts as pale as ashes, that stood at the feet of a bed, or walked over a church-yard by moonlight; and of others that had been conjured into the Red Sea, for disturbing people's rest, and drawing their curtains at midnight; with many other old women's fables of the like nature. As one spirit raised another, I observed that at the end of every story the whole company closed their ranks, and crowded about the fire. I took notice in particular of a little boy, who was so attentive to every story, that I am mistaken if he ventures to go to bed by himself this twelvemonth. Indeed, they talked so long, that the imaginations of the whole assembly were manifestly crazed, and, I am sure, will be the worse for it as long as they live. I heard one of the girls, that had looked upon me over her shoulder, asking the company how long I had been in the room, and whether I did not look paler than I used to do. This put me under some apprehensions that I should be forced to explain myself, if I did not retire; for which reason I took the candle in my hand, and went up into my chamber, not without wondering at this unaccountable weakness in reasonable creatures, that they should love to astonish and terrify one another. Were I a father, I should take particular care to preserve my children from those little horrors of imagination, which they are apt to contract when they are young, and are not able to shake off when they are in years. I have known a soldier, that has entered a breach, affrighted at his own shadow, and look pale upon a little scratching at his door, who the day before had marched up against a battery of cannon. There are instances of persons who have been terrified, even to distraction, at the figure of a tree, or the shaking of a bulrush. The truth of it is, I look upon a sound imagination as the greatest blessing of life, next to a clear judgment and a good conscience. In the mean time, since there are very few whose minds are not more or less subject to these dreadful thoughts and apprehensions, we ought to arm ourselves against them by the dictates of reason and religion, to *pull the old woman out of our hearts* (as Persius expresses it), and extinguish those impertinent notions which we imbibed at a time that we were not able to judge of their absurdity. Or, if we believe, as many wise and good men have done, that there are such phantoms and apparitions as those I have been speaking of, let us endeavour to establish to ourselves an interest in Him who holds the reins of the whole creation in his hand, and moderates them after such a manner, that it is impossible for one being to break loose upon another without his knowledge and permission.

"For my own part, I am apt to join in opinion with those who believe that all the regions of nature swarm with spirits; and that we have multitudes of spectators on all our actions, when we think ourselves most alone. But, instead of terrifying myself with such a notion, I am wonderfully pleased to think that I am always engaged with such an innumerable society, in searching out the wonders of the creation, and joining in the same concert of praise and adoration.

'——Nor think, though men were none,
That Heav'n would want spectators, God want praise:
Millions of spiritual creatures walk the earth
Unseen, both when we wake and when we sleep;
All these with ceaseless praise his works behold,
Both day and night. How often from the steep
Of echoing hill or thicket have we heard
Celestial voices to the midnight air,
Sole, or responsive each to other's note,
Singing their great Creator? Oft in bands,
While they keep watch, or nightly rounding walk,
With heav'nly touch of instrumental sounds,
In full harmonic number join'd, their songs
Divide the night, and lift our thoughts to heav'n.'—"

Another celebrated writer says—"Some are over credulous in these stories, others sceptical and distrustful, and a third sort perfectly infidel.

"Mr. Locke assures us, we have as clear an idea of spirit as of body. But, if it be asked, how a spirit, that never was embodied, can form to itself a body, and come up into a world where it has no right of residence, and have all its organs perfected at once; or how a spirit, once embodied, but now in a separate state, can take up its carcase out of the grave, sufficiently repaired, and make many resurrections before the last; or how the dead can counterfeit their own bodies, and make to themselves an image of themselves; by what ways and means, since miracles ceased, this transformation can be effected; by whose leave and permission, or by what power and authority, or with what wise design, and for what great ends and purposes, all this is done, we cannot easily imagine; and the divine and philosopher together will find it very difficult to resolve such questions.

"Before the Christian æra, some messages from the other world might be of use, if not necessary, in some cases, and on some extraordinary occasions; but since that time we want no new, nor can we have any surer, informations.

"Conscience, indeed, is a frightful apparition itself; and I make no question but it oftentimes haunts an oppressing criminal into restitution, and is a ghost to him sleeping or waking: nor is it the least testimony of an invisible world, that there is such a drummer as that in the soul, that can beat an alarm when he pleases, and so loud, as no other noise can drown it, no music quiet it, no power silence it, no mirth allay it, and no bribe corrupt it."

Inexhaustible are the opinions on this subject: therefore we shall conclude this Essay, and proceed to the more illustrative part of our work, without any further quotations; for various are the methods proposed by the learned for the laying of ghosts and apparitions. Artificial ones are easily quieted, if we only take them for real and substantial beings, and proceed accordingly. Thus, when a Friar, personating an apparition, haunted the apartment of the late Emperor Joseph, King Augustus, then at the Imperial court, flung him out of the window, and laid him upon the pavement so effectually, that he never rose or appeared again in this world.

THE
DOMINICAN FRIAR.

---

*An Extraordinary Event that happened
lately at Aix-la-Chapelle.*

As the following story, which is averred to be authentic, and to have happened very lately, may serve to shew, that the stories of this kind, with which the public are, from time to time, every now and then alarmed, are nothing more than artful impostures, it is presumed, it will be useful as well as entertaining to our readers to give it a place.

A person who kept a lodging-house near the springs at Aix-la-Chapelle, having lost his wife, committed the management of his family to his daughter, a sprightly, well-made, handsome girl, about twenty.

There were, at that time, in the house, two ladies and their waiting-woman, two Dutch officers, and a Dominican Friar.

It happened, that, as the young woman of the house was asleep one night in her bed, she was awakened by something that attempted to draw the clothes off the bed. She was at first frightened; but thinking, upon recollection, that it might be the house-dog, she called him by his name. The clothes, however, were still pulled from her; and she still imagining it was by the dog, took up a brush that lay in her reach, and attempted to strike him. At that moment she saw a flash of sudden light, that filled the whole room; upon which she shrieked out; all was again dark and silent, and the clothes were no longer drawn from her.

In the morning, when she related this story, every one treated it as a dream; and the girl herself at last took it for granted, that it was no more than an illusion.

The night following, she was again awakened by something that jogged her, and she thought she felt a hand in the bed; upon endeavouring to repress it, another flash of lightning threw her into a fit of terror: she shut her eyes, and crossed herself. When she ventured to open her eyes again, the light was vanished; but, in a short time, she felt what she supposed to be a hand again in the bed: she again endeavoured to repress it, and, looking towards the foot of the bed, saw a large luminous cross, on which was written distinctly, as with light, the words, "*Be Silent!*" She was now so terrified, that she had not power to break the injunction, but shrunk down into the bed, and covered herself over with the clothes.

In this situation she continued a considerable time; but, being again molested, she ventured once more to peep out, when, to her unspeakable astonishment, she saw a phantasm stand by the side of her bed, almost as high as the ceiling: a kind of glory encircled its head, and the whole was in the form of a crucifix, except that it seemed to have several hands, one of which again approached the bed.

Supposing the phenomenon to be some celestial vision, she exerted all her fortitude, and, leaping out of bed, threw herself upon her knees before it; but she instantly found herself assaulted in a manner which convinced her she was mistaken: she had not strength to disengage herself from something that embraced her, and therefore screamed out as loud as she could, to alarm the house, and bring somebody to her assistance.

Her shrieks awakened the ladies who lay in an adjacent chamber, and they sent their woman to see what was the matter. The woman, upon opening the room, saw a luminous phantasm, which greatly terrified her, and heard, in a deep threatening tone, the words—"*At thy peril be gone!*"

The woman instantly screamed out, and withdrew: the

ladies rose in the utmost consternation and terror, but nobody came to their assistance: the old man, the father of the girl, was asleep in a remote part of the house; the Friar also rested in a room at the end of a long gallery in another story; and the two Dutch officers were absent on a visit, at a neighbouring village.

No other violence, however, was offered to the girl that night. As soon as the morning dawned, she got up, ran down to her father, and told all that had happened: the two ladies were not long absent; they did not say much, but quitted the house. The Friar asked the girl several questions, and declared that he had heard other instances of the like nature, but said, the girl would do well to obey the commands of the vision, and that no harm would come of it. He said, he would remain to see the issue; and, in the mean time, ordered proper prayers and masses to be said at a neighbouring convent of his order, to which he most devoutly joined his own.

The girl was comforted with this spiritual assistance; but, notwithstanding, took one of the maids to be her bedfellow the next night. In the dead of the night, the flaming cross was again visible, but no attempt was made on either of the women. They were, however, greatly terrified; and the servant said, she would rather leave her place, than lie in the room again.

The Friar, the next morning, took the merit of the spirit's peaceable behaviour to himself. The prayers and masses were renewed, and application was made to the convents at Liege for auxiliary assistance. The good Friar, in the mean time, was by no means idle at home: he performed his devotions with great ardour, and towards evening bestowed a plentiful libation of holy water on the chamber and the bed.

The girl not being able to persuade the servant to sleep with her again in the haunted room, and being encouraged by the Friar to abide the issue, having also great confidence herself in the prayers, masses, and sprinklings, that had been used on the occasion, she ventured once more to sleep in the same room by herself.

In the night, after hearing some slight noises, she saw the room all in a blaze, and a great number of luminous crosses, with scraps of writing here and there very legible, among which the precept *to be silent* was most conspicuous.

In the middle of the room she saw something of a human appearance, which seemed covered only with a linen garment, like a shirt: it appeared to diffuse a radiance round it; and, at length, by a slow and silent pace, approached the bed.

When it came up to the bed-side, it drew the curtain more open, and, lifting up the bed-clothes, was about to come in. The girl, now more terrified than ever, screamed out with all her power. As every body in the house was upon the watch, she was heard by them all; but the father only had courage to go to her assistance, and his bravery was probably owing to a considerable quantity of reliques, which he had procured from the convent, and which he brought in his hand.

When he came, however, nothing was to be seen but some of the little crosses and inscriptions, several of which were now luminous only in part.

Being himself greatly terrified at these appearances, he ran to the Friar's apartment, and with some difficulty prevailed upon him to go with him to the haunted room. The Friar at first excused himself upon account of the young woman's being there in bed. As soon as he entered, and saw the crosses, he prostrated himself on the ground, and uttered many prayers and incantations, to which the honest landlord most heartily said *Amen*.

The poor girl, in the mean time, lay in a kind of trance; and her father, when the prayers were over, ran down stairs for some wine, a cordial being necessary to recover her: the Friar, at the same time, ordered him to light and bring with him a consecrated taper; for hitherto they had no light but that of the vision, which was still strong enough to discover every thing in the room.

In a short time the old man entered with a taper in his hand;

and in a moment all the luminous appearances vanished. The girl, soon after, recovered, and gave a very sensible account of all that had happened; and the landlord and the Friar spent the rest of the night together.

The Friar, however, to shew the power of the dæmon, and the holy virtue of the taper, removed it several times from the chamber, before the day broke, and the crosses and inscriptions were again visible, and remained so till the taper was brought back, and then vanished as at first.

When the sun arose, the Friar took his leave to go to matins, and did not return till noon. In the mean time the two Dutch officers came home, and soon learnt what had happened, though the landlord took all the pains he could to conceal it. The reports they heard were confirmed by the pale and terrified appearance of the girl; their curiosity was greatly excited, and they asked her innumerable questions. Her answers, instead of extinguishing, increased it. They assured the landlord, they would not leave his house, but, on the contrary, would afford him all the assistance in their power.

As they were young gentlemen of a military profession, and Protestants, they were at once bold and incredulous. They pretended, however, to adopt the opinion of the landlord, that the appearances were supernatural; but it happened that, upon going into the room, they found the remainder of the taper, on the virtues of which the landlord had so largely expatiated, and immediately perceived that it was only a common candle of a large size, which he had brought by mistake in his fright.

This discovery convinced them that there was a fraud, and that appearances that vanished at the approach of unconsecrated light must be produced by mere human artifice.

They therefore consulted together, and at length agreed, that the masses should be continued; that the landlord should not say one word of the candle, or the suspicions it had produced; that his daughter, the next night, should sleep in the apartment which had been quitted by the ladies; and that one of the officers should lie in the girl's bed, while the other, with the landlord, should wait in the kitchen, to see the issue.

This plan was accordingly, with great secrecy, carried into execution.

For two hours after the officer had been in bed, all was silent and quiet, and he began to suspect that the girl had either been fanciful, or that their secret had transpired: when, all on a sudden, he heard the latch of the door gently raised; and, perceiving something approach the bed and attempt to take up the clothes, he resisted with sufficient strength to frustrate the attempt, and immediately the room appeared to be all in a flame; he saw many crosses, and inscriptions enjoining silence and a passive acquiescence in whatever should happen; he saw also, in the middle of the room, something of a human appearance, very tall, and very luminous. The officer was at first struck with terror, and the vision made a second approach to the bed-side; but the gentleman, recovering his fortitude with the first moment of reflection, dexterously threw a slip knot, which he had fastened to one of the bed-posts, over the phantom's neck: he instantly drew it close, which brought him to the ground, and then threw himself upon him. The fall and the struggle made so much noise, that the other officer and the landlord ran up with lights and weapons; and the goblin was found to be no other than the good Friar, who, having conceived something more than a spiritual affection for his landlord's pretty daughter, had played this infernal farce, to gratify his passion.

Being now secured and detected, beyond hope of subterfuge or escape, he made a full confession of his guilt, and begged earnestly for mercy.

It appeared that this fellow, who was near six feet high, had made himself appear still taller, by putting upon his head a kind of *tiara* of embossed paper, and had also thrust a stick through the sleeves of his habit, which formed the appearance of a cross, and still left his hands at liberty; and that he had rendered himself and his apparatus visible in the dark by *phosphorus*.

The landlord contented himself with giving his reverence a hearty drubbing, and then turning him out of doors, with a strict injunction to quit the territory of Liege for ever, upon pain of being much more severely treated.

When it is considered, that it is but a few years ago, that a poor woman, within twenty miles of London, lost her life upon supposition that she was a witch; and that it is not many years since the Cock-lane ghost found advocates, even in the heart of London itself, among those who, before, were never accounted fools; it cannot but be useful to put down on record every imposition of this kind.

THE
SUPERSTITIOUS COUPLE.

In the letters from a gentleman on his travels in Italy to his friend in England, is the following curious account of an experiment tried with the Bolognian stone, of which phosphorus is made.

There was an English maid-servant in the house where we lodged, (observes this gentleman), and her bed-chamber was immediately over the one occupied by myself and friend. My companion having found his way into it, or, at least, supposing he had done so, wrote with some paste made merely with flour and water, the terrible words—"REMEMBER DEATH!" in great capitals, on the inside of the bed-curtains. Over the wet letters he strewed some of the crust prepared from this stone, which he had powdered for that purpose in a mortar; and, when he had so done, called me up, to see the words in letters of fire. We sat up for the discovery; but something very different from what we had expected, happened. The Italians are bigots, and consequently superstitious. It happened that the room, into which my friend had found his way, was not, as he imagined, that of the maid-servant, but of a couple of devout people, who accidentally slept in the house. We heard them undress; and followed our scheme, by getting on the upper stairs near the door of the room: we heard two voices, and we saw the candle on a table near the bed-side. The lady was first in bed; and the good man no sooner followed, than the candle was put out. On the instant of its extinction, appeared the terrible words. The lady screamed her prayers; the husband trembled over his Ave-Marias. The letters were absolutely fire, and the bed was not injured. The language was unintelligible to those who saw the words; and, perhaps, it was in that respect more terrifying, than if the admonition had been understood. The *Mene Tekel* of the prophet came into both their minds at once. They jumped out of bed, and alarmed the whole house. We were first in the room. My friend took occasion, in their confusion, to scrape off the whole matter very cleanly with his pocket knife. The company brought candles—there was nothing to be seen. Both husband and wife pointed to the place where the writing had appeared; but nothing but some smeared dirt was visible there. My friend kept his counsel, and the miracle was blazed all over Bologna the next day; and we left a legion of wondering priests in the house at our departure!

THE
HAUNTED BED-ROOM.

A young gentleman, going down from London to the west of England, to the house of a very worthy gentleman, to whom he had the honour to be related; it happened, that the gentleman's house was at that time full, by season of a kinswoman's wedding, that had lately been kept there. He therefore told the young gentleman, that he was very glad to see him, and that he was very welcome to him: "But, " said he, "I know not how I shall do for a lodging for you; for my cousin's marriage has not left a room free, save one, and that is haunted; but if you will lie there, you shall have a very good bed, and all other accommodations." "Sir, " replied the young gentleman, "you will very much oblige me by letting me lie there; for I have often coveted to be in a place that was haunted." The gentleman, very glad that his kinsman was so well pleased with his accommodations, ordered the chamber to be got ready, and a good fire to be made in it, it being winter-time. When bed-time came, the young gentleman was conducted up into his chamber, which, besides a good fire, was furnished with all suitable accommodations; and, having recommended himself to the Divine protection, went to bed. Lying some time awake, and finding no disturbance, he fell asleep; out of which, however, he was awaked about three o'clock in the morning, by the opening of the chamber-door, and the entrance of somebody in the appearance of a young woman, having a night-dress on her head, and only her shift on: but he had no perfect view of her, for his candle was burnt out; and though there was a fire in the room, yet it gave not light enough to see her distinctly. But this unknown visitant going to the chimney, took the poker, and stirred up the fire; by the flaming light whereof, he could discern the appearance of a young gentlewoman more distinctly; but whether it was flesh and blood, or an airy phantom, he knew not. This appearance having stood some time before the fire, as if to warm itself, at last walked two or three times about the room, and then came to the bed-side; where having stood a little while, she took up the bed-clothes, and went into bed, pulling the bed-clothes upon her again, and lying very quietly. The young gentleman was a little startled at this unknown bed-fellow; and, upon her approach, lay on the further side of the bed, not knowing whether he had best rise or not. At last, lying very still, he perceived his bed-fellow to breathe; by which guessing her to be flesh and blood, he drew nearer to her, and taking her by the hand, found it warm, and that it was no airy phantom, but substantial flesh and blood; and finding she had a ring on her finger, he took it off unperceived. The gentlewoman being all this while asleep, he let her lie without disturbing her, and patiently waited the result of this singular situation. He had not long remained in suspense, when his fair companion hastily flung off the bed-clothes again, and getting up, walked three or four times about the room; as she had done before; and then, standing awhile before the door, opened it, went out, and shut it after her. The young gentleman, perceiving by this in what manner the room was haunted, rose up, and locked the door on the inside; and then lay down again, and slept till morning; at which time the master of the house came to him, to know how he did, and whether he had seen any thing, or not? He told him, that an apparition had appeared to him, but begged the favour of him that he would not urge him to say any thing further, till the whole family were all together. The gentleman complied with his request, telling his young friend, that, having found him well, he was perfectly satisfied.

The desire the whole family had to know the issue of this affair, made them dress with more expedition than usual, so that there was a general assembly of the gentlemen and ladies before eleven o'clock, not one of them being willing to appear in dishabille. When they were all got together in the great hall, the young gentleman told them, he had one favour to desire of the ladies before he would say any thing, and that was, to know whether either of them had lost a ring? The young gentlewoman, from whose finger it was taken, having missed it all the morning, and not knowing how she lost it, was glad to hear of it again, and readily owned she wanted a ring. The young gentleman asked her if that was it, giving it into her hand, which she acknowledging to be her's, and thanking him, he turned to his kinsman, the master of the house—"Now Sir, " said he, "I can assure you, " (taking the gentlewoman by the hand) "this is the lovely spirit by which your chamber is haunted."—And thereupon repeated what is related.

I want words to express the confusion the young gentlewoman seemed to be in at this relation, who declared herself perfectly ignorant of all that he said; but believed it might be so, because of the ring, which she perfectly well remembered she had on when she went to bed, and knew not how she had lost it.

This relation gave the whole company a great deal of diversion; for, after all, the father declared, that since his daughter had already gone to bed to his kinsman, it should be his fault if he did not go to bed to his daughter, he being willing to bestow her upon him, and give her a good portion. This generous offer was so advantageous to the young gentleman, that he could by no means refuse it; and his late bed-fellow, hearing what her father had said, was easily prevailed upon to accept him for her husband.

REMARKABLE INSTANCE
OF THE
POWER OF IMAGINATION.

It has been remarked, that when the royal vault is opened for the interment of any of the royal family, Westminster Abbey is a place of great resort: some flock thither out of curiosity, others to indulge their solemn meditations.

By the former of these motives it was, when the royal vault was opened for the interment of her illustrious Majesty Queen Caroline, that five or six gentlemen who had dined together at a tavern were drawn to visit that famous repository of the titled dead. As they descended down the steep descent, one cried—"It's hellish dark;" another stopped his nostrils, and exclaimed against the nauseous vapour that ascended from it; all had their different sayings. But, as it is natural for such spectacles to excite some moral reflections, even with the most gay and giddy, they all returned with countenances more serious than those they had entered with.

Having agreed to pass the evening together, they all went back to the place where they dined; and the conversation turned on a future state, apparitions, and some such topics. One among them was an infidel in those matters, especially as to spirits becoming visible, and took upon him to rally the others, who seemed rather inclinable to the contrary way of thinking. As it is easier to deny than to prove, especially where those that maintain the negative will not admit any testimonies which can be brought against their own opinion, he singly held out against all they had to alledge. To end the contest, they proposed to him a wager of twenty guineas, that, as great a hero as he pretended, or really imagined himself, he had not courage enough to go alone at midnight into the vault they had seen that day. This he readily accepted, and was very merry with the thoughts of getting so much money with such ease. The money on both sides was deposited in the hands of the master of the house; and one of the vergers was sent for, whom they engaged, for a piece of gold, to attend the adventurer to the gate of the cathedral, then shut him in, and wait his return.

Every thing being thus settled, the clock no sooner struck twelve, than they all set out together; they who laid the wager being resolved not to be imposed on by his tampering with the verger. As they passed along, a scruple arose, which was, that though they saw him enter the church, how they should be convinced he went as far as the vault; but he instantly removed their doubts, by pulling out a pen-knife he had in his pocket, and saying, "This will I stick into the earth, and leave it there; and if you do not find it in the inside of the vault, I will own the wager lost." These words left them nothing to suspect; and they agreed to wait at the door his coming out, believing he had no less stock of resolution than he had pretended: it is possible, the opinion they had of him was no more than justice.

But, whatever stock of courage he had, on his entrance into that antique and reverend pile, he no sooner found himself shut alone in it, than, as he afterwards confessed, he found a kind of shuddering all over him, which, he was sensible, proceeded from something more than the coldness of the night. Every step he took was echoed by the hollow ground; and, though it was not altogether dark, the verger having left a lamp burning just before the door that led to the chapel (otherwise it would have been impossible for him to have found the place), yet did the glimmering it gave, rather add to, than diminish, the solemn horror of every thing around.

He passed on, however; but protested, had not the shame of being laughed at, prevented him, he would have forfeited more than twice the sum he had staked to have been safe out again.

At length he reached the entrance of the vault: his inward terror increased; yet, determined not to be overpowered by fear, he descended; and being come to the last stair, stooped forwards, and struck the pen-knife with his whole force into the earth. But, as he was rising in order to quit so dreadful a place, he felt something pluck him forward; the apprehension he before was in, made an easy way for surprise and terror to seize on all his faculties: he lost in one instant every thing that could support him, and fell into a swoon, with his head in the vault, and part of his body on the stairs.

Till after one o'clock his friends waited with some degree of patience, though they thought he paid the titled dead a much longer visit than a living man could choose. But, finding he did not come, they began to fear some accident: the verger, they found, though accustomed to the place, did not choose to go alone; they therefore went with him, preceded by a torch, which a footman belonging to one of the company had with him. They all went into the Abbey, calling, as they went, as loud as they could: no answer being made, they moved on till they came to the vault; where, looking down, they soon perceived what posture he was in. They immediately used every means they could devise for his recovery, which they soon effected.

After they got him out of the Abbey to the fresh air, he fetched two or three deep groans; and, in the greatest agitation, cried, "Heaven help me! Lord have mercy upon me!" These exclamations very much surprised them; but, imagining he was not yet come perfectly to his senses, they forbore farther questions, till they had got him into the tavern, where, having placed him in a chair, they began to ask how he did, and how he came to be so indisposed. He gave them a faithful detail, and said, he should have come back with the same sentiments he went with, had not an unseen hand convinced him of the injustice of his unbelief. While he was making his narrative, one of the company saw the pen-knife sticking through the fore-lappet of his coat. He immediately conjectured the mistake;

and, pulling out the pen-knife before them all, cried out, "Here is the mystery discovered: for, in the attitude of stooping to stick the knife in the ground, it happened, as you see, to go through the coat; and, on your attempting to rise, the terror you was in magnified this little obstruction into an imaginary impossibility of withdrawing yourself, and had an effect on your senses before reason had time to operate." This, which was evidently the case, set every one, except the gentleman who had suffered so much by it, into a roar of laughter. But it was not easy to draw a single smile from him: he ruminated on the affair, while his companions rallied and ridiculed this change in him: he well remembered the agitations he had been in. "Well, " replied he; when he had sufficiently recovered, "there is certainly something after death, or these strange impulses could never be. What is there in a church more than in any other building? what in darkness more than light, which in themselves should have power to raise such ideas as I have now experienced? Yes, " continued he, "I am convinced that I have been too presumptuous: and, whether spirits be or be not permitted to appear, that they exist, I ever shall believe."

THE
WESTMINSTER SCHOLARS.

A few years since, some Westminster scholars received great insult from a hackney-coachman, who treated them with the greatest scurrility, because they would not comply with an overcharge in his fare. This behaviour the youths did not forget, and were resolved to punish him without danger of prosecution;

upon which one of them devised the following whimsical turn of revenge.

Four of these gentlemen, one dark evening, about nine o'clock, (having previously learned where his coach would be) called him from off the stand, and desired the coachman to drive over Westminster Bridge to Newington. They had not long been seated, when one of them, with a sportive tone of voice, said, "Come, boys, let us begin."

They then instantly dressed themselves in black clothes, and every necessary befitting mourners at a funeral, (which articles they brought with them in small parcels.) And the night was particularly favourable for carrying their scheme into execution: for it was uncommonly dark, and *very still*. 'Twas such a night that Apollonius Rhodius thus describes—

> "Night on the earth pour'd darkness; on the sea,
> The wakesome sailor to Orion's star
> And Helice turn'd heedful. Sunk to rest,
> The traveller forgot his toil; his charge,
> The centinel; her death-devoted babe,
> The mother's painless breast. The village dog
> Had ceas'd his troublous bay: each busy tumult
> Was hush'd at this dread hour; and darkness slept,
> Lock'd in the arms of silence."

To terrify him the more, they wore linen hat-bands and scarfs, instead of crape. And when they had got into the loneliest part of St. George's Fields (for at that time they were not built over as at present), they called to him, and desired him to stop, as they wanted to get out.

They marked the side the coachman came to open the door of; and he that sat next the other door, opened it at the same instant.

What the coachman felt on seeing the first mourner move out with the greatest solemnity, can be better conceived than expressed: but what were his terrors when the second approached him, a majestic spare figure about six feet perpendicular, who passed him (as did the first) without speaking a word.

As fast as one youth got out, he went round to the other side of the coach, stepped in, and came out a second time at the opposite door.

In this manner they continued, till the coachman, if he had the power of counting, might have told forty.

When they had thus passed out seemingly to the number of twenty, the poor devil of a coachman, frightened almost to death, fell upon his knees, and begged for mercy's sake the King of Terrors would not suffer any more of his apparitions to appear; for, though he had a multitude of sins to account for, he had a wife and a large family of children, who depended upon his earnings for support.

The tallest of these young gentlemen then asked him, in a hoarse tone of voice, what was his heaviest sin? He replied, committing his lodger, a poor carver and gilder, to the Marshalsea, for rent due to him, which the badness of the times, and his business in particular, would not enable him to pay. He said, he would not have confined him so long, but in revenge for a severe beating he gave him one day when they fell to loggerheads and boxed. He further told them, the poor man had been six months in captivity; and that he understood from a friend of his, the other day, that he made out but a miserable living by making brewers' pegs, bungs for their barrels, and watchmakers' skewers.

The young gentleman then told him, that if he did not instantly sign his discharge, which he would write, he might rest assured of no mitigation of the dreadful punishment he would go through in a few minutes; for those he had seen come out of his coach were his harpies in disguise, and were now in readiness to bear him to the infernal regions.

The trembling villain, without the least hesitation, complied. One of the scholars fortunately having a pen and ink, the King of Terrors wrote the discharge in a fair leaf of his pocket-book, as well as he could in the dark, and then made the coachman sign it.

Having so done, the scholars told him he might go for the present, and that he would find his coach in less than an hour in Piccadilly or Oxford Street.

One of the youths then mounted the box, while the others got within, and away they drove to the Marshalsea, but in the way they stopped till they had taken off their disguise.

The youth who had the discharge, after making a collection among the others, went into the prison, and gave the poor fellow what set him at liberty the next morning.

The scholars then drove on to Oxford Street, congratulating themselves on the success of their adventure, and all happy to a degree of rapture at being instrumental in obtaining the captive's liberty.

About a quarter of an hour after they quitted the coach, they observed the coachman arrive; who mounted the box, and drove home, muttering the bitterest execrations, and damning his father confessor for bilking him of half a guinea which he gave him that morning for an absolution, that was to have rubbed out the entire score of his transgressions.

THE
IDEOT'S FUNERAL.

The following extraordinary affair happened about ten years since, at a village in the north of England.

About midnight, the minister of the parish was not a little alarmed at hearing the church bell tolling. He immediately dispatched one of his servants for the beadle, to inquire into the cause of this wonderful event; who, when he came, appeared to be under more dreadful apprehensions than the clergyman himself. However, the result of their deliberations was, that, in order to be certainly informed of the truth and ground of the matter, they should go forward to the church: but, on their way, what served considerably to increase their fears, was their seeing a light within the church. The great bell gave over tolling, and was succeeded, in its turn, by the little, or handbell (commonly used in that country at funerals), which, in a short time, also became silent. On their near approach to the church, they discovered, by the help of the light within, the *mort-cloth* moving up and down the area thereof. Though this last part of the dreadful scene might have been sufficient to intimidate persons possessed of no ordinary degree of courage; yet such was the bravery and resolution of the Reverend Doctor, that he even ventured to accost the nocturnal disturber of their repose: when, on lifting up the *mort-cloth*, to his inexpressible surprise, he discovered the terrible apparition to be only an unhappy young man belonging to the parish, who had for some time past been disordered in his senses, and who had got into the church by some secret means or other, and, as the good Doctor readily conjectured, was amusing himself in this manner, by the representation of a funeral: a case not at all unlikely, as ideots in general are remarkably fond of any thing relative to a funeral procession.

THE
VENTRILOQUIST.

The following anecdote is related by Adrianus Turnibis, the greatest critic of the sixteenth century, and who was admired and respected by all the learned in Europe.

"There was a crafty fellow," says he, "called Petrus Brabantius, who, as often as he pleased, would speak from his stomach, with his mouth indeed open, but his lips unmoved, of which I have been repeatedly an eye and ear witness. In this manner he put divers cheats on several persons: amongst others, the following was well known.

"There was a merchant of Lyons, lately dead, who had acquired a great estate by unjust dealings. Brabantius happening to be at Lyons, and hearing of this, comes one day to Cornutus, the son and heir of this merchant, as he walked in a portico behind the church-yard, and tells him that he was sent to inform him of what was to be done by him; and that it was more requisite to think about the soul and reputation of his father, than thus wander about the church-yard, lamenting his death. In an instant, while they were thus discoursing, a voice was heard, as if it was that of the father, though, in reality, it proceeded from his own stomach. Brabantius seemed terribly affrighted. The voice informed the son the state his father was in by reason of his injustice, what tortures he endured in purgatory, both on his own, and his son's account, whom he had left heir of his ill-gotten goods: that no freedom was to be expected by him, till just expiation was made by giving alms to such as stood most in need, and that these were the Christians who were taken by the Turks: that he should put entire confidence in the man who was by special providence now come to him, and give him money, to be employed by religious persons for the ransom of so many as were captives at Constantinople. Cornutus, who was a good sort of a man, yet loth to part with his money, told Brabantius that he would advise upon it; and desired he would meet him in the same place the next day. In the mean time, he began to suspect there might be some fraud in the place, as it was shady, dark, and fit for echoes or other delusions. The next day, therefore, he takes him to an open plain, where there was neither bush nor briar; but there, notwithstanding all his precaution, he hears the same story, with this addition, that he should forthwith deliver Brabantius six thousand franks, and purchase three masses daily to be said for him, or else the miserable soul of his father could not be freed. Cornutus, though thus bound by conscience, duty, and religion, yet with reluctance delivered him the money, without taking any receipt, or having any witness to the payment of it. Having thus dismissed him, and hearing no more of his father, he became somewhat more pleasant than he had been since his father's death. One day this change in him was observed by some friends, who were at dinner at his house; upon which he told them what had befallen him: when his friends so derided him, one and all, for his credulity, in being so simply cheated of his money, that, for mere grief and vexation, within a few days after, he died."

THE
FEMALE FANATIC,
AND HEAVENLY VISITOR.

The following curious affair happened a few years since at Paris, and is well attested by a gentleman of the greatest respectability.

A widow-lady, aged about sixty-two, who lodged in a two-pair-of-stairs floor, in the *Rue de la Ferronnerie*, with only a maid-servant, was accustomed to spend several hours every day at her devotions, before the altar dedicated to St. Paul, in a neighbouring church. Some villains observing her extreme bigotry, resolved (as she was known to be very rich) to share her wealth. Therefore one of them took the opportunity to conceal himself behind the carved work of the altar; and when no person but the old lady was in the church, in the dusk of the evening, he contrived to throw a letter just before her. She took it up, and not perceiving any one near her, supposed it came by a miracle; which she was the more confirmed in, when she saw it was signed, *Paul the Apostle*, and purported, "The satisfaction he received by her addressing her prayers to him, at a time when so many new-canonized saints engrossed the devotion of the world, and robbed the primitive saints of great part of their wonted adoration; and, to shew his regard for his devotee, said, he would come from Heaven, with the angel Gabriel, to sup with her, at eight in the evening."

It is scarcely credible to think any one could be deceived by so gross a fraud: but to what length of credulity, will not superstition carry the weak mind! The infatuated lady believed it all; and rose from her knees in a transport, to prepare the entertainment for the heavenly guests she expected.

When the supper was bespoke, and the sideboard set out to the best advantage, she thought that her own plate (which was worth near four hundred pounds sterling) did not make so elegant a shew as she desired; therefore sent to her brother (who was a Counsellor of the Parliament of Paris) to borrow all his plate; charging her maid not to tell the occasion, but only, that she had company to supper, and should be obliged to him if he would lend her his plate for that evening. The Counsellor was surprised at this message, as he knew the frugality of his sister's way of life; and suspected that she was enamoured with some fortune-hunter, who might marry her for her fortune, and thereby deprive the family of what he expected at his sister's death: therefore he absolutely refused to send the plate, unless the maid would tell him what guests she expected. The girl, alarmed for her mistress's honour, replied, that her pious lady had no thoughts of a husband; but that, as St. Paul had sent her a letter from heaven, saying, that he and the *Angel Gabriel* would come to supper with her, her mistress wanted to make the entertainment as elegant as possible. The Counsellor, who knew the turn of his sister's mind, immediately suspected some villains had imposed on her; and sent the maid directly with the plate, while he went to the Commissary of the quarter, and gave him this information. The magistrate accompanied him to a house adjoining, from whence they saw, just before eight o'clock, a tall man, dressed in long vestments, with a white beard, and a young man in white, with large wings at his shoulders, alight from a hackney-coach, and go up to the widow's apartment. The Commissary immediately ordered twelve of the foot *guet* (the guards of Paris) to post themselves on the stairs, while he himself knocked at the door, and desired admittance. The old lady replied, that she had company, and could speak to no one. But the Commissary answered, that he must come in: for that he was St. Peter, and had come to ask St. Paul and the Angel, how they came out of heaven without his knowledge. The divine visitors were astonished at this, not expecting any more Saints to join them: but the lady, overjoyed at having so great an apostle with her, ran eagerly to the door; when the Commissary, her brother, and the *guet*, rushing in, presented their musquets, and seized her guests, whom they immediately carried to the Chatelot.

On searching the criminals, two cords, a razor, and a pistol, were found in St. Paul's pocket; and a gag in that of the feigned angel. Three days after, their trial came on: when, in their defence, they pleaded, that the one was a soldier of the French foot-guards, and the other a barber's apprentice; and that they had no other evil design, but to procure a good supper for themselves at the expence of the widow's folly; that, it being carnival time, they had borrowed the above dresses; that the soldier had found the two cords, and put them into his pocket; the razor was what he used to shave himself with; and the pistol was to defend himself from any insults so strange a habit might expose him to, in going home. The barber's apprentice said, his design also was only diversion; and that, as his master was a tooth-drawer, the gag was what they sometimes used in their business. These excuses, frivolous as they were, were of some avail to them; and, as they had not manifested any evil design by an overt act, they were acquitted.

But the Counsellor, who had foreseen what would happen, through the insufficiency of evidence, had provided another stroke for them. No sooner were they discharged from the civil power, but the Apparitor of the Archbishop of Paris seized them, and conveyed them to the Ecclesiastical Prison; and, in three days more, they were tried and convicted of a scandalous profanation, by assuming to themselves the names, characters, and appearances, of an holy apostle and a blessed angel, with an intent to deceive a pious and well-meaning woman, and to the scandal of religion. On this they were condemned to be publicly whipped, burnt on the shoulder by a hot iron, with the letters G.A.L. and sent to the galleys for fourteen years.

The sentence was executed on them the next day, on a scaffold in the *Place de Greve*, amidst an innumerable crowd of spectators: many of whom condemned the superstition of the lady, when perhaps they would have shewn the same on a like occasion; since, it may be supposed, that if many of *their* stories of apparitions, of saints, and angels, had been judiciously examined, they would have been found, like the above, to be either a gross fraud, or the dreams of an over-heated, enthusiastic imagination.

I shall make no reflections on the above fact; but leave it to the impartial consideration of the reader.

THE
FEMALE SPRITES.

In September 1764, the following extraordinary incident happened in the family of a clergyman then living in Bartholomew Close.

The gentleman and his wife returning home about eleven o'clock from a friend's house, where they had been to spend the evening, desired the maid to get them warm water to mix with some wine. There being no fire in the parlour, they went into the kitchen; and while the water was heating, the gentleman ordered the maid to get a pan of coals, and warm the bed. The servant had not long been gone up stairs, when the gentleman and his wife heard an uncommon noise over their heads, like persons walking without shoes: and, presently after, a woman enters the kitchen, without any other clothes on than her shift and cap. Their astonishment at such a sight so greatly frightened them, that they had neither of them power to speak a word: and while they were thus absorbed in amazement, another woman entered the room in like manner. Just at this time the maid came down from warming the bed; and, though greatly surprised at so unexpected an appearance, had the courage to ask them who they were? and what they wanted? To which they replied, that they were servants at their next-door neighbour's, and, being awakened out of their sleep by their master's calling out, Fire and thieves! ran up stairs, and entering the garret window, came down, to preserve themselves from danger, and procure assistance. Upon this, inquiry being made, the gentleman's daughter at the adjoining house was found in violent fits, which occasioned his calling the maids hastily to her assistance; and this caused an alarm that had nearly proved fatal to the clergyman's wife, who was, at that time, far gone with child.

THE
PRUSSIAN DOMINO,
OR
FATAL EFFECTS OF JEALOUSY.

An officer of rank in the service of the late King of Prussia, having lost an amiable wife whom he tenderly loved, became quite inconsolable. Deeply wounded with his affliction, his mind was so absorbed in melancholy, that the transient pleasures of life were no longer a delight to him; he retired from the court and the field, and at once secluded himself from all society.

Among the numerous friends who lamented his excessive

sorrow, his Monarch was not the least, who endeavoured to soothe his distracted mind with sympathetic tenderness. Indeed, his Majesty considered him not only an agreeable companion, but a valuable friend; and was so much interested in his behalf, that he was determined, if possible, to divert his immoderate grief. But neither the promises of promotion, or the threats of disgrace, could draw him from his retirement. At length, after many zealous efforts had proved ineffectual, a plan was suggested by the King himself, which promised success. His Majesty resolved to give a masquerade, to which, by inviting Lindorf (for that was the officer's name), an opportunity might be again taken to entice him within that circle of gaiety, of which he was once the admiration. The invitation being accompanied with an affectionate and earnest solicitation from the King, Lindorf could not refuse accepting the offer; and, on the evening appointed, he was once more seen in the rooms of splendour and festivity. On his entrance he met the King, who, after greeting him with great kindness, began to rally him upon his late weakness. Lindorf thanked his Majesty for the honour he did him, and, after a short reply, they for some time walked up and down the saloon together; when at length it was agreed to part, that each might amuse himself according to his own liking, with the different characters exhibited that evening. But the King's intention was solely to watch the movements of Lindorf; for with heartfelt regret he beheld, as they parted, the fixed melancholy that still brooded on his countenance: and, when he beheld him pass, with downcast eyes, the saloon, where the dance and music reigned with such irresistible sway, all hope of reclaiming the unhappy widower disappeared. For some time he was witness of his melancholy deportment, and was much affected to find that, where every face beamed a smile, the countenance of Lindorf alone was sad and dejected. The King, despairing of his project being successful, was about to quit the rooms, when he beheld Lindorf suddenly stop and speak to a lady in a black domino. Rejoiced at this circumstance, hope again revived, and he stayed his departure, to watch the event.

Lindorf, when he quitted the King, continued to walk up and down the rooms, nothing attracting his attention but the lady in the black domino, who, wherever he turned, always appeared before him. At first he imagined the character intended merely to amuse him, and that her strange deportment was instigated by his friends; but the unusual solemnity attending her appearance, after he had in vain desired her to desist, struck him with astonishment. He suddenly stopped, and demanded who she was? "I dare not tell you, " answered the domino, in a deep and plaintive tone of voice. Lindorf startled—his blood ran cold; it was exactly the voice of his deceased wife. "Who are you? for heaven's sake, tell me, or I die!" exclaimed Lindorf. "You will be more wretched than you are, if I tell you, " replied the mysterious unknown, in accents that doubly excited his curiosity. "Tell me, " said he, "I conjure you; for I cannot be more wretched than I now am. Tell me all, and do not leave me in this state of inquietude." "Know then, " answered the domino, "I am your wife." Lindorf started—every nerve was wrung with anguish. "Impossible, " said he in a fright, "it cannot be; yet the voice appears the same." Here his tongue faltering, he ceased to speak. When he had somewhat recovered his recollection, he ejaculated, "In the name of God, do tell me who you are? Is it a trick, or do I dream?" "Neither, " replied the unknown; and continued, in the same tone of voice, to describe several particulars relative to his family, and in what manner many things were placed in the drawers belonging to his deceased wife, which none but himself and the departed knew of. At length he was convinced the figure before him must be the apparition of his wife; and, in the voice of anguish and despair, requested she would unmask and let him see her face. That the figure refused to do, saying, that would be a sight he could not bear. "I can bear any thing, " he replied, "but the pain your denial creates. I entreat you, let me see your face; do not refuse me!" Again she denied him; till at last, by repeated entreaties, and his promises not to be alarmed, she consented to unmask, and desired him to follow her into an anti-room, solemnly charging him not to give way to his feelings. They then proceeded to the adjoining room.

The King, who was an eye-witness of the deep conversation they were engaged in, beheld, with rapture, their entrance into the anti-chamber, and saw the door closed. "He is certainly restored, " said the Monarch to his confidential attendant; "Lindorf is most assuredly saved; he has made an appointment with some pretty woman, and has just retired to enjoy a private conversation. In her endearments he will, I hope, forget his sorrows. So we may now partake of the festivities of the evening." Saying which, he immediately joined the motley group with great cheerfulness.

Lindorf felt his blood chill, as the door of the anti-chamber closed; but, the warmth of affection returning, he no sooner entered, than he claimed the dreadful promise. Again, in the most solemn manner, she advised him not to urge that which might tend to his misery, as she was certain he had not sufficient fortitude to endure a sight of her. With horror he heard the remonstrance; and the solemnity of her deportment only inspired his eager curiosity the more. At length, after many strict injunctions, she lifted up the mask; when the astonished Lindorf beheld the most horrid spectacle of a skeleton head. "Oh, God!" he exclaimed, and, groaning, fell senseless on the floor. In vain the mysterious domino attempted to recover him. Sorrow had for a long time preyed upon his existence, and terror had now for ever quieted the unhappy Lindorf. He breathed no more; he was a lifeless corpse. Instantly the domino quitted the room, and retired from the masquerade.

The King had just returned to his post of observation, and saw the domino depart. In vain he waited for Lindorf to follow; an hour expired, and no Lindorf appeared. This raised the curiosity of the Monarch. The door was left partly open, and he resolved to enter; when, to his great surprise and sorrow, he beheld Lindorf stretched on the floor, a corpse. He instantly alarmed the company; but the mystery of his death in vain they attempted to develope. No marks of violence appeared on his body, which was the more astonishing; and, to add to the mystery, the masqued lady was not to be found in any of the rooms. Messengers were then dispatched, and advertisements distributed, all over the city of Berlin, offering large rewards for her apprehension; but no further information could be gained, than that deposed by two chairmen, who affirmed, they brought the domino to the rooms, which from their account only added to the mystery.

Their declaration was as follows—"Having received a letter, enjoining secrecy, and desiring them to attend in the dusk of the evening, at a certain church porch, to carry a lady to the masquerade; they, thinking it was some person who intended to play the character of a hobgoblin, or sprite, did not hesitate, and made no farther inquiry, but proceeded, at the hour appointed, to the place mentioned; where they found a person waiting in a black domino, just as the advertisement described. On their arrival, without speaking a word, the domino placed the money for hire in their hands, and instantly entered the chair, which they immediately conveyed to the masquerade. On their arrival, without uttering a word, she darted from them into the crowd, and they saw no more of her until twelve o'clock, when, on passing the door, they discovered the domino again seated in the chair. They were much surprised at such strange conduct; but, without reflecting on the event, they conveyed her back again, as was agreed, to the same church porch, when they received a further gratuity, and departed." Such was the deposition of the two chairmen, at once mysterious and incomprehensible. This intelligence still more astonished the King, who in vain used every method to make further discovery in this extraordinary and unhappy affair.

Several years elapsed, without any thing occurring that

could lead to a developement of this dreadful catastrophe. All search after the lady was now given up, and nothing but the remembrance of the unhappy affair remained. At length the hour arrived, when this dreadful mystery was explained, which displayed one of the most diabolical and desperate transactions ever known. The particulars are as follow.

A lady, then at the point of death, requested to see some confidential friend of the King's; which request was immediately complied with: to whom she made the following confession. In accents scarcely audible, she told them, she was the person who appeared in the black domino, in so mysterious a manner, to Lindorf, and which unhappily caused his death. That revenge for neglected love instigated her to play the part she did; but that she had no idea the consequence would have been so fatal: her intention being merely to assume the appearance of his deceased wife, in order that she might upbraid him, and gratify her revenge for having broke his vow in marrying her sister instead of herself; and also that she might effectually persuade him to desist from his melancholy intentions of remaining a widower, and prevail on him to marry her—for although he refused her request personally, yet she imagined the scheme must be successful, when played off under the appearance of a spirit of his deceased wife; and, to deceive his imagination, she had endeavoured to personify her; for which purpose she had procured the head of a skeleton, and assumed that character which had proved the death of the man she so ardently loved, and the source of endless misery to herself. She then related the conversation that had passed between them on that fatal evening, and fully described the whole particulars of that mysterious affair. She likewise acknowledged she endeavoured to imitate the voice of his deceased wife; and declared her intention for having the chair brought to the church porch was to render the proceeding the more mysterious and incomprehensible in case of a scrutiny. On concluding this melancholy tale, she fetched a deep sigh, and instantly expired.

THE
DEAD MAN AND
ANATOMICAL PROFESSOR.

Many, who were personally acquainted with Mr. Junker, have frequently heard him relate the following anecdote.

Being Professor of Anatomy, he once procured, for dissection, the bodies of two criminals who had been hanged. The key of the dissecting room not being immediately at hand, when they were carried home to him, he ordered them to be laid down in a closet which opened into his own apartment. The evening came; and Junker, according to custom, proceeded to resume his literary labour before he retired to rest. It was now near midnight, and all his family were fast asleep, when he heard a rumbling noise in his closet. Thinking that, by some mistake, the cat had been shut up with the dead bodies, he arose, and, taking the candle, went to see what had happened. But what must have been his astonishment, or rather his panic, on perceiving that the sack which contained the two bodies was rent through the middle. He approached, and found that one of them was gone.

The doors and windows were well secured, and he thought it impossible the bodies could have been stolen. He tremblingly looked round the closet, and observed the dead man seated in a corner.

Junker stood for a moment motionless: the dead man seemed to look towards him; he moved both to the right and left, but the dead man still kept his eyes upon him.

The Professor then retired, step by step, with his eyes still fixed upon the object of his alarm, and holding the candle in his hand, until he reached the door. The dead man instantly started up, and followed him. A figure of so hideous an appearance, naked, and in motion—the lateness of the hour—the deep silence which prevailed—every thing concurred to overwhelm him with confusion. He let fall the only candle which he had burning, and all was darkness. He made his escape to his bed-chamber, and threw himself on the bed: thither, however, he was pursued; and he soon felt the dead man embracing his legs, and loudly sobbing. Repeated cries of "Leave me! leave me!" released Junker from the grasp of the dead man; who now exclaimed, "Ah! good executioner! good executioner! have mercy upon me."

Junker soon perceived the cause of what had happened, and resumed his fortitude. He informed the re-animated sufferer who he really was, and made a motion, in order to call up some of the family. "You wish then to destroy me, " exclaimed the criminal. "If you call any one, my adventure will become public, and I shall be taken and executed a second time. In the name of humanity, I implore you to save my life."

The physician struck a light, decorated his guest with an old night-gown, and, having made him take off a cordial, requested to know what had brought him to the gibbet. It would have been a truly singular exhibition, observed Junker, to have seen me, at that late hour, engaged in a *tête-à-tête* with a dead man decked out in a night-gown.

The poor wretch informed him, that he had enlisted as a soldier, but that, having no great attachment to the profession, he had determined to desert; that he had unfortunately entrusted his secret to a kind of crimp, a fellow of no principle, who recommended him to a woman, in whose house he was to remain concealed: that this woman had discovered his retreat to the officers of police, &c.

Junker was extremely perplexed how to save the poor man. It was impossible to retain him in his own house, and keep the affair a secret; and to turn him out of doors, was to expose him to certain destruction. He therefore resolved to conduct him out of the city, in order that he might get into a foreign jurisdiction; but it was necessary to pass the gates of the city, which were strictly guarded. To accomplish this point, he dressed the man in some of his old clothes, covered him with a cloak, and, at an early hour, set out for the country, with his *protegé* behind him. On arriving at the city gate, where he was well known, he said in a hurried tone, that he had been sent for to visit a sick person who was dying in the suburbs. He was permitted to pass. Having both got into the open fields, the deserter threw himself at the feet of his deliverer, to whom he vowed eternal gratitude; and, after receiving some pecuniary assistance, departed, offering up prayers for his happiness.

Twelve years after, Junker, having occasion to go to Amsterdam, was accosted on the Exchange by a man well-dressed and of the best appearance, who, he had been informed, was one of the most respectable merchants in that city. The merchant, in a polite manner, inquired whether he was not Professor Junker of Halle; and, on being answered in the affirmative, he requested, in an earnest manner, his company to dinner. The Professor consented. Having reached the merchant's house, he was shewn into an elegant apartment, where he found a beautiful wife, and two fine healthy children: but he could scarcely suppress his astonishment at meeting with so cordial a reception from a family with whom, he thought he was entirely unacquainted.

After dinner, the merchant, taking him into his counting-room, said, "You do not recollect me?"—"Not at all."—"But I well recollect you; and never shall your features be effaced from my remembrance. You are my benefactor. I am the person who came to life in your closet, and to whom you paid so much attention. On parting from you, I took the road to Holland. I wrote a good hand, was tolerably expert at accounts; my figure was somewhat interesting; and I soon obtained employment as a merchant's clerk. My good conduct, and my zeal for the interests of my patron, procured me his confidence, and his daughter's love. On his retiring from business, I succeeded him, and became his son-in-law. But for you, however, I should not have lived to experience all these enjoyments. Henceforth, look upon my house, my fortune, and myself, as at your disposal."

Those who possess the smallest portion of sensibility can easily represent to themselves the feelings of Junker.

THE
DRUNKEN BUCKS,
AND CHIMNEY-SWEEP.

On March the 19th, 1765, four bucks assembled at an inn in Grantham, to drink a glass, and play a game of cards. The glass circulating very briskly, before midnight they became so intoxicated, that not one of them was able to determine how the game stood; and several disputes, interspersed with a considerable number of oaths, ensued, till they agreed to let the cards lie, and endeavour to drink themselves sober. Shortly after they resumed the game; and each man imagining himself capable of directing the rest, they soon came again to very high words; when the waiter, fearful that some bad consequences might ensue, let them know it was near three o'clock, and, if any gentleman pleased, he would wait on him home. Instead of complying with his request, the geniuses looked upon it as an indignity offered them, and declared, with the most horrid imprecations, that not one of them would depart till day-light. But, in the height of their anger, an uncommon noise in the chimney engaged their attention; when, on looking towards the fire-place, a black spectre made its appearance, and crying out in a hollow menacing tone—"*My father has sent me for you, infamous reprobates!*" They all, in the greatest fright, flew out of the room, without staying to take their hats, in broken accents confessing their sins, and begging for mercy.

It appears, that the master of the inn, finding he could not get rid of his troublesome guests, and having a chimney-sweeper in his house sweeping other chimneys, he gave the boy directions to descend into the room as above related, whilst he stood at a distance, and enjoyed the droll scene of the bucks' flight.

THE
CRIPPLEGATE GHOST.

———————————

The following story, well authenticated in the neighbourhood of Cripplegate, will convince the reader, that vicious intentions are sometimes productive of much good to the parties they intended to injure.

A gentlewoman in that parish, having lain for some days in a trance, was at length laid out and buried for dead, with a gold ring on her finger. The sexton knowing thereof, he and his wife, with a lanthorn and candle, went privately the next night, and dug up the coffin, opened it, untied the winding sheet, and was going to cut off her finger for the sake of the valuable ring buried with her, they not being otherwise able to remove it; when, suddenly, the lady raised herself up (being just then supposed miraculously to come out of her trance). The sexton and his wife ran away in a horrible fright, leaving their lanthorn behind them; which the lady took up, and made haste home to her house. When knocking hard at the door, the maid-servant asked who was there? "'Tis I, your mistress, " replied the lady; "and do, for God's sake, let me in immediately, as I am very cold." The maid, being much surprised and terrified at this reply, neglected to open the door, ran away to her master, and acquainted him with the circumstance; who would scarcely believe her tale, till he went himself to the door, and heard his wife relate the dreadful particulars. He immediately let her in, put her into a warm bed; and, by being well looked after, she soon perfectly recovered, and lived to have three children afterwards.

This extraordinary resuscitation is conjectured, by the faculty, to have been occasioned by the sudden circulation of the blood on the villain's attempting to cut off the finger.

A monument, with a curious inscription of this affair, is still to be seen in Cripplegate church.

THE
VENTRILOQUIST.

The following anecdotes are related by the Abbé de la Chapelle, of the French Academy.

This gentleman, having heard many surprising circumstances related concerning one Monsieur St. Gille, a grocer, at St. Germain-en-Laye, near Paris, whose astonishing powers as a ventriloquist had given occasion to many singular and diverting scenes, formed the resolution to see him. Struck by the many marvellous anecdotes related concerning him, the Abbé judged it necessary first to ascertain the truth by the testimony of his own senses, and then to inquire into the cause and manner in which the phenomena were produced.

After some preparatory and necessary steps (for Monsieur St. Gille had been told he did not chuse to gratify the curiosity of every one), the Abbé waited upon him, informed him of his design, and was very cordially received. He was taken into a parlour on the ground floor; when Monsieur St. Gille and himself sat on the opposite sides of a small fire, with only a table between them, the Abbé keeping his eyes constantly fixed on Monsieur St. Gille all the time. Half an hour had passed, during which that gentleman diverted the Abbé with a relation of many comic scenes which he had given occasion to by this talent of his; when, all on a sudden, the Abbé heard himself called by his name and title, in a voice that seemed to come from the roof of a house at a distance. He was almost petrified with astonishment: on recollecting himself, however, he asked Monsieur St. Gille whether he had not just then given him a specimen of his art? He was answered only by a smile. But while the Abbé was pointing to the house from which the voice had appeared to him to proceed, his surprise was augmented on hearing himself answered, "It was not from that quarter, " apparently in the same kind of voice as before, but which now seemed to issue from under the earth, at one of the corners of the room. In short, this factitious voice played, as it were, every where about him, and seemed to proceed from any quarter or distance from which the operator chose to transmit it to him. The illusion was so very strong, that, prepared as the Abbé was for this kind of conversation, his mere senses were absolutely incapable of undeceiving him. Though conscious that the voice proceeded from the mouth of Monsieur St. Gille, that gentleman appeared absolutely mute while he was exercising this talent; nor could the author perceive any change whatever in his countenance. He observed, however, at this first visit, that Monsieur St. Gille contrived, but without any affectation, to present only the profile of his face to him, while he was speaking as a ventriloquist.

The next experiment made was no less curious than the former, and is related as follows—

Monsieur St. Gille, returning home from a place where his business had carried him, sought for shelter from an approaching thunder-storm, in a neighbouring convent. Finding the whole community in mourning, he inquires the cause, and is told, that one of their body had lately died, who was the ornament and delight of the whole society. To pass away the time, he walks into the church, attended by some of the religious, who shew him the tomb of their deceased brother, and speak feelingly of the scanty honours they had bestowed on his memory. Suddenly, a voice is heard, apparently proceeding from the roof of the choir, lamenting the situation of the deceased in purgatory, and reproaching the brotherhood with their lukewarmness and want of zeal on his account. The friars, as soon as their astonishment gave them power to speak, consult together, and agree to acquaint the rest of the community with this singular event, so interesting to the whole society.

Monsieur St. Gille, who wished to carry on the deception still farther, dissuaded them from taking this step; telling them, that they will be treated by their absent brethren as a set of fools and visionaries. He recommended to them, however, the immediately calling the whole community into the church, when the ghost of their departed brother may, probably, reiterate his complaints. Accordingly, all the friars, novices, lay-brothers, and even the domestics of the convent, are immediately summoned and collected together. In a short time, the voice from the roof renewed its lamentations and reproaches; and the whole convent fell on their faces, and vowed a solemn reparation. As a first step, they chaunted a *De Profundis* in full choir; during the intervals of which, the ghost occasionally expressed the comfort he received from their pious exercises and ejaculations on his behalf. When all was over, the Prior entered into a serious conversation with Monsieur St. Gille; and, on the strength of what had just passed, sagaciously inveighed against the absurd incredulity of our modern sceptics, and pretended philosophers, as to the existence of ghosts or apparitions. Monsieur St. Gille thought it now high time to undeceive the good fathers. This purpose, however, he found extremely difficult to effect, till he had prevailed upon them to return with him into the church, and there be witnesses of the manner in which he had conducted this ludicrous deception.

In consequence of these memoirs, presented by the author to the Royal Academy of Sciences at Paris, in which he communicated to them the observations that he had collected on the subject of ventriloquism in general, and those he had made on Monsieur St. Gille in particular; that learned body deputed two of its members, M. de Fouchy and Le Roi, to accompany him to St. Germain-en-Laye, in order to verify the facts, and to make their observations on the nature and causes of this extraordinary faculty. In the course of this inquiry, a very singular plan was laid and executed, to put Monsieur St. Gille's powers of deception to the trial, by engaging him to exert them in the presence of a large party, consisting of the commissaries of the Academy, and some persons of the highest quality, who were to dine in the open forest near St. Germain-en-Laye on a particular day. All the members of this party were in the secret, except a certain lady, here designated by the title of the Countess de B. who was pitched upon as a proper person for Monsieur St. Gille's delusive powers, as she knew nothing either of him or of ventriloquism; and possibly for another reason, which the Abbé, through politeness, suppresses. She had been told in general, that this party had been formed in consequence of a report, that an aërial spirit had lately established itself in the forest of St. Germain-en-Laye; and that a grand deputation from the Academy of Sciences was to pass the day there, to inquire into the reality of the fact.

Monsieur St. Gille was one of the first of this select party; and, previous to his joining the company in the forest, he completely deceived one of the Commissaries of the Academy, who was then walking apart from the rest, and whom he accidentally met. Just as he was abreast of him, prepared and guarded as the academician was against a deception of this kind, he verily believed that he heard his associate M. de Fouchy, who was then with the company at above an hundred yards distance, calling after him to return as expeditiously as possible. His valet, too, after repeating to his master the purport of M. de Fouchy's supposed acclamation, turned about towards the company, and, with the greatest simplicity imaginable, bawled out as loud as he could, in answer to him, "Yes, Sir."

After this promising beginning, the party sat down to dinner; and the aërial spirit, who had been previously furnished with proper anecdotes respecting the company, soon began to address the Countess of B. particularly, in a voice that seemed to be in the air over their heads. Sometimes he spoke to her from the tops of the trees around them, or from the surface of the ground, but at a great distance; and at other times seemed to speak from a considerable depth under her feet. During the dinner, the spirit appeared to be absolutely inexhaustible in the gallantries he addressed to her; though he sometimes said civil things to the rest of the company. This kind of conversation lasted above two hours; and, in fine, the Countess was firmly persuaded, as the rest of the company affected to be, that this was the voice of an aërial spirit: nor would she, as the author affirms, have been undeceived, had not the rest of the company, by their unguarded behaviour, at length excited in her some suspicions. The little plot against her was then owned; and she acknowledged herself to be mortified only in being awakened from such a pleasing delusion.

Several other instances of Monsieur St. Gille's talents are related. He is not, however, the only ventriloquist now in being. The author, in the course of his inquiries on this subject, was informed that the Baron de Mengin, a German nobleman, possessed this art in a very high degree. The Baron has also constructed a little puppet, or doll, (the lower jaw of which he moves by a particular contrivance), with which he holds a spirited kind of dialogue. In the course of it, the little virago is so impertinent, that at last he thrusts her into his pocket; from whence she seems, to those present, to grumble, and complain of her hard treatment. Some time ago, the Baron, who was then at the court of Bareith, being in company with the Prince de Deux Ponts, and other noblemen, amused them with this scene. An Irish officer, who was then present, was so firmly persuaded that the Baron's doll was a real living animal, previously taught by him to repeat these responses, that he watched his opportunity at the close of the dialogue, and suddenly made an attempt to snatch it from his pocket. The little doll, as if in danger of being suffocated, during the struggle occasioned by this attempt, called out for help, and screamed incessantly from the pocket till the officer desisted. She then became silent; and the Baron was obliged to take her out from thence, to convince him, by handling her, that she was a mere piece of wood.

It should have been observed, at the beginning of the Abbé's anecdotes, that ventriloquism is the art of vocal deception. It is an art, or quality, possessed by certain persons, by means of which they are enabled to speak inwardly, having the power of forming speech by drawing the air into the lungs, and to modify the voice in such a manner as to make it seem to proceed from any distance, or in any direction whatever.

There is no doubt but many of these deceptions have been magnified by weak people into those dreadful stories of apparitions and hobgoblins, which the credulous and enthusiastic are too apt implicitly to believe.

THE
SCHOOL-BOY APPARITION.

A few years since, the inhabitants of Dorking, in Surrey, entertained a notion, that a ghost walked in a certain place in that neighbourhood; and that she (for it was an ancient lady, lately dead) was seen hovering about the mansion-house, which was left uninhabited for some time; that she would be up and down in the house very often in the day-time, making a rumbling and a clattering noise; and in the night-time she walked in the neighbouring fields, with a candle in her hand, and though the wind blew ever so hard, it would not blow the candle out; that sometimes she would appear in the open fields, sometimes up in the trees; and, in particular, there was a little heath near Dorking, called Cotman Dean, where, it was said, she was frequently seen.

There was a boarding-school of boys in that town, some of whom were particularly roguish, and contrived all this walking, from the beginning to the end. First, they got a small rope; and, tying one end of it to an old chair which stood in an upper room of the house (for they had found the means to get in and out of the house at pleasure), they brought the other end of the rope down on the other side of the house, in a private place, where it could not easily be seen; and by this they pulled the old chair up, and then let it fall down again: this made a great noise in the house, and was heard distinctly by many of the neighbours. Then other boys of the same gang took care to call out the old women in the next houses, that now they might hear the old lady playing her pranks; and, accordingly, they would all assemble in the court-yard, where they could plainly hear the noises, but not one of them would venture to go up stairs. If any one offered to go a little way up, then all was quiet; but, as soon as ever they retired, the rumbling would begin again. This was the day's deception.

In the night, one of these unlucky boys got a dark lanthorn, which was a thing, at that time, the country-people did not understand; and with this he walked about the orchard, and two or three closes near the house, shewing the light in different directions. His comrades would then call all the old women about them to see it. Then, on a sudden, the light would seem to go out, as the boy closed up the lanthorn. Then he would run swiftly across the whole field, and shew his light again on the other side. Now he would be up in a tree, then in the road, then upon the middle of the heath; so that the country-people made no more question, but that the old lady walked with a candle in her hand, and that they saw the light of it; in a word, it passed for an apparition, and was generally conceived as such by the neighbourhood, till the knavery was discovered, the boys punished, and the towns-people laughed at for their credulity.

THE
CREDULOUS PEASANTS.

No longer ago than the year 1788, when the husbandmen of Paris suffered so severely by the devastation on the 13th of July in that year, many of the farmers were positively so superstitious at their own created fears, that, notwithstanding considerable sums were offered to indemnify them for their losses, and to encourage them to carry on with spirit the cultivation of their lands, with new seeds, new implements, &c. they peremptorily refused, on account of a foolish report that was then prevalent in some parts of the country where the storm happened. They said, that two giants were seen peeping out of the clouds, and threatening, with terrible countenances, gigantic frowns, and high-sounding words, that they would return next year on the same thirteenth day of July, with a greater scourge than they then felt. Terrified either at the imagined report, or at the fancied sight of the giants (which terror and a weak brain will often produce), many of the unhappy sufferers abandoned their houses, and commenced beggars, rather than return to the labours of the field: so great was their affright, in consequence of that tremendous storm.

This story, though hardly credible, may be depended on as a fact, and may be seen in many of the public prints of that time.

THE
NOCTURNAL DISTURBERS.

The following authentic story is related by Dr. Plot, in his Natural History of Oxfordshire.

Soon after the murder of King Charles the First, a commission was appointed to survey the King's house at Woodstock, with the manor, park, woods, and other demesnes thereunto belonging; and one Collins, under a feigned name, hired himself as Secretary to the Commissioners: who, upon the thirteenth of October 1849, met, and took up their residence in the King's own rooms. His Majesty's bed-chamber they made their kitchen; the council-hall, their pantry; and the presence-chamber was the place where they sat for the dispatch of business. His Majesty's dining room they made their wood-yard, and stored it with the wood of the famous royal oak, from the high park; which, that nothing might be left with the name of the King about it, they had dug up by the roots, and split, and bundled up into faggots for their firing.

Things being thus prepared, they sat on the 16th of the same month for the dispatch of business; and in the midst of their first debate, there entered a large black dog, as they thought, which made a dreadful howling, overturned two or three of their chairs, and then crept under a bed, and vanished. This gave them the greater surprise, as the doors were kept constantly locked, so that no real dog could get in or out. The next day, their surprise was increased; when, sitting at dinner in a lower room, they heard plainly the noise of persons walking over their heads, though they well knew the doors were all locked, and there could be nobody there. Presently after, they heard also all the wood of the King's oak brought by parcels from the dining-room, and thrown with great violence into the chamber; as also the chairs, stools, tables, and other furniture, forcibly hurled about the room; their own papers of the minutes of their transactions torn; and the ink-glass broken. When this noise had some time ceased, Giles Sharp, their Secretary, proposed to enter first into these rooms; and, in presence of the Commissioners, of whom he received the key, he opened the doors, and found the wood spread about the room, the chairs tossed about, and broken, the papers torn, and the ink-glass broken (as has been said); but not the least track of any human creature, nor the least reason to suspect one, as the doors were all fast, and the keys in the custody of the Commissioners. It was therefore unanimously agreed, that the power who did this mischief must have entered the room at the key-hole.

The night following, Sharp, the Secretary, with two of the Commissioners' servants, as they were in bed in the same room (which room was contiguous to that where the Commissioners lay), had their beds' feet lifted so much higher than their heads, that they expected to have their necks broken; and then they were let fall at once with so much violence, as shook the whole house, and more than ever terrified the Commissioners.

On the night of the nineteenth, as all were in bed in the same room for greater safety, and lights burning by them, the candles in an instant went out with a sulphurous smell: and, that moment, many trenchers of wood were hurled about the room; which, next morning, were found to be the same their Honours had eaten off the day before, which were all removed from the pantry, though not a lock was found opened in the whole house. The next night, they fared still worse: the candles went out as before; the curtains of their Honours' beds were rattled to and fro with great violence; their Honours received many cruel blows and bruises by eight great pewter dishes, and a number of wooden trenchers, being thrown on their beds, which being heaved off were heard rolling about the room, though in the morning none of them were to be seen. The following night, likewise, they were alarmed with the tumbling down of oaken billets about their beds, and other frightful noises: but all was clear in the morning, as if no such thing had happened. The next night, the keeper of the King's house and his dog lay in the Commissioners' room; and then they had no disturbance. But, on the night of the twenty-second, though the dog lay in the room as before, yet the candles went out, a number of brickbats fell from the chimney into the room, the dog howled piteously, their bed-clothes were all stripped off, and their terror increased. On the twenty-fourth night, they thought all the wood of the King's oak was violently thrown down by their bed-sides; they counted sixty-four billets that fell, and some hit and shook the beds in which they lay: but in the morning none were found there, nor had the door been opened where the billet-wood was kept. The next night, the candles were put out, the curtains rattled, and a dreadful crack like thunder was heard; and one of the servants, running to see if his master was not killed, found three dozen of trenchers laid smoothly under the quilt by him.

But all this was nothing to what succeeded afterwards. The twenty-ninth, about midnight, the candles went out; something walked majestically through the room, and opened and shut the windows; great stones were thrown violently into the room, some of which fell on the beds, others on the floor; and, about a quarter after one, a noise was heard, as of forty cannon discharged together, and again repeated at about eight minutes distance. This alarmed and raised all the neighbourhood; who, coming into their Honours' rooms, gathered up the great stones, fourscore in number, and laid them in the corner of a field, where, in Dr. Plot's time, who reported this story, they were to be seen. This noise, like the discharge of cannon, was heard through all the country for sixteen miles round. During these noises, which were heard in both rooms together, the Commissioners and their servants gave one another over for lost, and cried out for help; and Giles Sharp, snatching up a sword, had well nigh killed one of their Honours, mistaking him for the spirit, as he came in his shirt, from his own room to their's. While they were together, the noise was continued, and part of the tiling of the house was stripped off, and all the windows of an upper room were taken away with it.

On the thirtieth at midnight, something walked into the chamber, treading like a bear; it walked many times about, then threw a warming-pan violently on the floor: at the same time a large quantity of broken glass, accompanied with great stones and horses' bones, came pouring into the room, with uncommon force; these were all found in the morning, to the astonishment and terror of the Commissioners, who were yet determined to go on with their business.

But, on the first of November, the most dreadful scene of all ensued. Candles in every part of the house were lighted up, and a great fire made. At midnight, the candles all yet burning, a noise, like the burst of a cannon, was heard in the room, and the burning billets were tossed about by it even into their Honours' beds, who called Giles and his companions to their relief, otherwise the house had been burned to the ground. About an hour after, the candles went out as usual; the crack of as many cannon was heard; and many pailfuls of green stinking water were thrown upon their Honours' beds; great stones were thrown in, as before; the bed-curtains and bedsteads torn and broken; the windows shattered; and the whole neighbourhood alarmed with the most dreadful noises; nay, the very rabbit-stealers that were abroad that night in the warren, were so terrified, that they fled for fear, and left their ferrets behind them. One of their Honours, this night, spoke; and, in the name of God, asked what it was? and why it disturbed them so? No answer was given to this, but the noise ceased for a while; when the spirit came again, and, as they all agreed, brought with it seven devils worse than itself. One of the servants now lighted a large candle, and placed himself in the doorway between the two chambers, to see what passed; and, as he watched, he plainly saw a hoof striking the candle and candlestick into the middle of the room, and afterwards making three scrapes over the snuff, scraped it out. Upon this the same person was so bold as to draw a sword; but he had scarce got it out, when he felt an invisible hand had hold of it too, and pulled with him for it, and, at length prevailing, struck him so violently on the head with the hilt, that he fell down for dead with the blow. At this instant was heard another burst, like the discharge of the broadside of a ship of war; and, at about a minute or two's distance each, no less than nineteen more such. These shook the house so violently, that they expected every moment it would fall upon their heads. The neighbours, on this, as has been said, being all alarmed, flocked to the house in great numbers, and all joined in prayer and psalm-singing; during which the noise still continued in the other rooms, and the report of cannon was heard, as from without, though no visible agent was seen to discharge them.

But what was the most alarming of all, and put an end to their proceedings effectually, happened the next day, as they were all at dinner; when a paper, in which they had signed a mutual agreement to reserve a part of the premises out of the general survey, and afterwards to share it equally amongst them, (which paper they had hid, for the present, under the earth, in a pot in one corner of the room, in which an orange-tree grew), was consumed in a wonderful manner, by the earth's taking fire, with which the pot was filled, and burning violently with a blue flame, and an intolerable stench, so that they were all driven out of the house, to which they could never again be prevailed upon to return.

This wonderful contrivance was all the invention of the memorable Joseph Collins, of Oxford, otherwise called *Funny Joe*; who, having hired himself for their Secretary, under the name of Giles Sharp, by knowing the private traps belonging to the house, and the help of *pulvis fulminans* and other chemical preparations, and letting his fellow-servants into the scheme, carried on the deceit, without discovery, to the very last, so dextrously, that the late Dr. Plot, in his Natural History, relates the whole for fact, in the gravest manner.

MARESCHAL SAXE,
AND
THE HAUNTED CASTLE.

The following very remarkable adventure, which befel the Mareschal de Saxe, whilst returning to his country-seat, near

Dresden, in Saxony, has often been related by him to his friends and acquaintance; and, as the Mareschal was not less famed for his love of truth, than for his heroic courage as a warrior, none of them ever doubted the truth of his relation.

"Returning, " says the Mareschal, "from the fatigues of a very active campaign to my country-seat, in order to seek, in retirement, some relaxation during the remainder of the winter, I arrived on the third day at a small village, on the verge of an extensive forest. At about half a league from this village, stood an ancient castle, in which some of the country-people were usually wont to take up their abode, and from which they had of late been driven, according to their account, by the nightly appearance of a most terrific spectre, whose visit was announced by the most hideous groans. On conversing with some of the villagers, " observes the Mareschal, "I found that an universal terror pervaded the whole neighbourhood; many of them declaring they had actually seen the dreadful ghost; whilst others, taking their declaration for granted, promulgated the story, according as their imaginations were more or less affected by their fears.

"Willing, if possible, to comfort these poor people, and to convince them that their senses were deceived, I told them they were wrong to suffer their fears to get the better of their reason; and that, if any of them had the courage to examine more closely into the affair, they would find the whole was nothing more than some imposture, or the effusion of a superstitious brain, or, at most, a trick played upon them by some wicked people on purpose to amuse themselves by sporting with their feelings. But I was much disappointed to find that my arguments had but little effect. I therefore determined, if possible, to trace the affair to the bottom before I departed, in order to dispel their fears, and do away the unfavourable impression they had so generally entertained of the castle being haunted.

"I now told them, I would pass a night in one of the apartments of the castle, provided I were furnished with a bed, and other necessaries requisite for such an undertaking. 'Moreover, ' said I, 'if this ghostly personage should honour me with a visit, I shall not fail to propose articles of accommodation between you.' To this they readily assented, and seemed much pleased with my proposition.

"In the evening, my bed, fire, and other requisites, being ready, I was conducted to my new abode; on entering which, I proposed to some of my conductors to pass the night with me, which they, one and all, declined, under various pretences. 'Well then, my good people, ' said I, rallying their want of courage, 'the day is now closing apace, I would have you return immediately, lest this nightly intruder should intercept you in your retreat.' Whereupon my companions took leave, and hastened with all speed from the castle.

"Being now alone, I thought it prudent to examine the castle with the most minute circumspection. After various researches to discover all the private avenues of the place, I returned to the apartment I proposed sleeping in, at the further end of which I perceived a door that till now I had not discovered. I essayed to open it, but in vain, as it was fastened on the other side. This naturally excited my suspicion. I again made the attempt, and again was unsuccessful. I then prepared to guard myself against a surprise; I therefore charged my pistols, and laid them together with my sword in a convenient place to seize them on the least alarm. I then took a slight repast, of such provisions as had been prepared for me; after which I amused myself, until my usual hour of going to rest, with examining the Gothic decorations of my apartment, and then laid me down on the bed, and, being rather overcome with the fatigue of the day, I soon sunk into a profound sleep. How long I continued in this state, I cannot exactly say; but I conjectured it to be about midnight, when I was alarmed with the most unaccountable noise I had ever heard. I listened a few seconds, to ascertain from whence the sound came, and soon found it proceeded from without the door I had fruitlessly attempted to open. I instantly jumped from the bed, seized my arms, and was in the act of advancing towards it, determined to find out the cause of this disturbance, let what would be the consequence; when, suddenly the door flew open, with the most tremendous crash. A hollow groan issued from the vaults below; and a tall figure of gigantic appearance, clad in complete armour, rose to my view. The figure's appearance was so sudden and terrific, that I could not in a moment collect myself sufficiently to call out and speak to it; but, a moment after, my courage returned, and, calling to mind, that I could only find safety in my own courageous efforts, and not doubting but the intruder was a mortal like myself, I instantly levelled one of my pistols, and fired. The ball struck the breast-plate of the figure, glided quickly off, and lodged in the wall. I levelled again, fired, and with the same effect. I then drew my sword, at the same time exclaiming, 'Know that I am the Mareschal de Saxe; that I am a stranger to fear, and that this sword shall quickly prove whether thou art mortal or not!' 'Be thou the Mareschal de Saxe, or the devil, ' replied the figure; 'thy courage here can avail thee nought. I have the means to destroy thee, or an hundred such, in an instant. But, follow me; thy obedience only can insure thy safety.' I now saw that resistance would be vain, as several figures clad in armour like the first, and well armed, appeared at each door. 'Well then, ' said I, 'since it is so, lead the way; but remember, that the first who dares touch me dies, if my own life is the immediate forfeiture.'

"We then quitted the apartment, by the secret door already mentioned; and, descending by a circuitous flight of stairs, soon arrived at another door, which flew open on our approach. No sooner were we entered, than my guide gave a signal to those who followed, and the door was instantly shut. A number of Vulcan-like creatures now appeared, bearing lighted torches, and leading the way through a winding subterraneous passage. We soon came to a spacious arched vault, in which I beheld upwards of fifty persons very actively engaged in the various processes of coining. The whole mystery was now developed; and I discovered that, for the first time in my life, I had fallen into the hands of a most desperate gang of coiners. Escape was now utterly impossible; nor could I entertain the most distant hope of succour from without the castle, as my sudden disappearance would rather operate to confirm the terror of the villagers, than stimulate them to search after me.

"The man in armour now turned to me, and addressed me in nearly the following words—'You now see for what purpose we are here arrived. I am the chief of this band; and it is principally to me you may attribute your preservation. We have but recently taken up our abode in this castle; and the plan we have fallen upon to terrify the villagers and country round, and thereby keep them from pursuing us, has hitherto succeeded beyond our most sanguine expectations; nor was it likely we should have been disturbed for years to come, had you not visited these parts. Of your resolute intention to sleep in the haunted apartment we were informed by our friends without; your name also was made known to us; upon which an universal consternation ensued. Many wished to fly, in order to avoid, what they conceived, inevitable destruction: others were of opinion, it would be better to suffer you to enter the castle quietly; and as, most likely you would be attended with but few persons, to dispatch you all in the night, and hide your bodies among the ruins in one of the vaults. This last proposition had the majority; as it was considered, that our own safety would not only be secured for the present by this act, but it would in all probability prevent others from making the like attempt hereafter. But this proceeding was happily over-ruled by me and a few others—I say, happily; for though we are considered, in the eye of the law, as co-brothers with assassins and midnight robbers, yet God forbid that we should add to our crimes by staining our hands with the blood of the innocent. To be brief, I promised that, with the aid of a few of my companions, I would drive you from the castle by the same stratagem I have before made use of to others, or, if that did not succeed, to secure and conduct you by force. Thus have I explained the cause of your present detention. The regaining your liberty must entirely depend on your acquiescence with our proposals; and there is a way I can point out, by which you may secure both your own safety and our's.' 'Name it not then, ' said I, interrupting him, 'if it be dishonourable; for I had rather perish here by your hands, than owe my liberty to any connivance at your iniquities, or be the instrument of your future security!' 'Use your own pleasure, ' continued he, in a determined tone of voice; 'but you certainly must not depart this place until you have bound yourself by your *honour* not to divulge a secret, on which depend the lives of so many persons. That word, once pledged by the Mareschal de Saxe, will be a sufficient guarantee of our future safety. I could have wished our request had been more congenial to your feelings; but our situation is desperate, and consequently impels us to enforce, what we would, under all other circumstances, have solicited as the least of favours—your word of honour.

"I paused for several minutes: a confused murmur now run throughout the whole place, and an universal disapprobation at the chief's forbearance began now to manifest itself. Add to which, I saw the utter impracticability of escape without complying with their demand; and I knew that their prepossession in my favour was but partial, and of course might soon give way to their former plan of assassinating me for their safety. If I continued inflexible, I perceived my death was inevitable. Therefore, as the majority were favourably inclined, I made a virtue of necessity, and gave them my word to keep the secret of the whole affair locked within my own breast. 'You are now at liberty, ' said the chief, 'to return to your apartment, where you may rely on being perfectly safe until break of day, when you had better depart.' Whereupon the doors flew open, and I was conducted back to my old lodging, where I sat ruminating on the strangeness of the adventure.

"Day now appearing, I quitted the castle, and hied me to the village, where I found most of the inhabitants already in waiting, eager to hear how I made out with the ghost. Numberless were their interrogatories, which I only answered by telling them I was not at liberty to disclose what I had seen and heard. Their old opinions were now more fully confirmed than ever; and, I believe, from that moment none have had courage to venture near the castle after dark; and it is probable that, to this day, the whole mystery has never been truly explained to their satisfaction. Shortly after, I set out on my journey, and soon arrived in safety at my own domain.

"About four years after this, a person rode up to my gate, leading a couple of beautiful chargers, which he delivered, with a letter addressed to me, into the hands of my domestics; and, having so done, he clapped spurs to his horse, and disappeared in an instant. On opening the letter, I found it contained nearly the following words—

'*From the pretended Ghost of the Haunted Castle, to the Mareschal de Saxe.*

'Brave Mareschal—You are now at liberty to divulge the secret of our affair in the haunted castle. Our fortunes are now made; and, ere you receive this, we shall be far from hence. But remember, that whatever the world may say as to the propriety of keeping your word with men like us, know, that the honour of a prince[A], once pledged, should be kept inviolate, even though given in a bad cause. My companions desired me to beg your acceptance of the horses you will receive herewith, as a mark of their most grateful acknowledgments. Adieu! May you live long, and be happy.'—"

FOOTNOTES:

[A]The Mareschal was the son of a King.

REMARKABLE RESUSCITATION.

In the first volume of the *Causes Célèbres*, a popular French work, is the following extraordinary story, which occasioned a serious law-suit.

Two men in trade, who lived in the street St. Honoré in Paris, nearly equal in circumstances, both following the same profession, and united in the closest friendship, had each of them a child, much about the same age. These children were brought up together, and conceived a mutual attachment, which, ripening with years into a stronger and more lively sentiment, was approved by the parents on both sides. This young couple was upon the point of being made happy, by a more solemn union, when a rich financier, conceiving a passion for the young maiden, unfortunately crossed their inclinations by demanding her in marriage. The allurements of a more brilliant fortune seduced her father and mother, notwithstanding their daughter's repugnance, to consent to the change. To their entreaties, however, she was obliged to yield, and sacrificed her affections by becoming the wife of the financier. Like a woman of virtue, she forbade her earlier lover the house. A fit of melancholy, the consequence of this violence done to her inclinations by entering into an engagement of interest, brought on her a malady, which so far benumbed her faculties, that at length she was given over by the faculty, apparently died, and was accordingly laid out for burial.

Her former lover, who had once before beheld her in a similar situation, flattered himself that he might possibly again find her in a trance. This idea not only suspended his grief, but prompted him to bribe the grave-digger, by whose aid he dug up the body in the night-time, and conveyed it home. He then used every means in his power for recalling her to life, and was overjoyed on discovering that his endeavours were not ineffectual.

It is not easy to conceive the surprise of the young woman on her resuscitation, when she found herself in a strange house, and, as it were, in the arms of her lover, who soon informed her of what had taken place on her account. She then comprehended the extent of her obligation to her deliverer; and love, more pathetic than all his persuasions to unite their destinies, determined her, on her recovery, to escape with him into England. This was effected; and they lived for some years in the closest union.

At the end of ten years, they conceived the natural wish of revisiting their own country, and at length returned to Paris, where they took no precaution whatever of concealing themselves, being persuaded that no suspicion would attach to their arrival. It happened however, by chance, that the financier met his wife in one of the public walks. The sight of her made so strong an impression on him, that for some time he imagined it must be her apparition; and, being fully persuaded of her death, he could not for a long time efface that idea. However, he so contrived it as to join her; and, notwithstanding the language she made use of to impose upon him, he left her with the conviction that he was not deceived at finding her a living substance.

The singularity of this event gave more charms to the woman in the eyes of her former husband than she before possessed. He therefore acted with such address, that he discovered her abode, notwithstanding all her precautions, and reclaimed her with all the regular formalities of justice.

It was in vain that the lover maintained the right which his cares for his mistress gave him to the possession of her; that he represented her inevitable death but for him; that his adversary divested himself of all his own rights, by causing her to be buried; that he ought even to be accused of homicide, for want of having taken proper precautions to assure himself of her death; and a thousand other ingenious reasons, which love suggested to him. But, finding that the judicial ear was unfavourable, and not thinking it expedient to wait the result of a definitive judgment, he fled with his mistress into a foreign country; where they passed the remainder of their days without further molestation.

THE
CREDULOUS BISHOP.

A few years since, a memorable conference took place between Dr. Fowler (then Bishop of Gloucester) and a Mr. Justice Powell: the former, a zealous defender of ghosts; and the latter, somewhat sceptical about them. They had several altercations upon the subject; and once, when the Bishop made a visit to the Justice, the latter, contracting the muscles of his face into an air of more than usual severity, assured the Bishop, that, since their last disputation, besides his Lordship's strong reasons, he had met with no less proof than ocular demonstration, to convince him of the real existence of ghosts. "How!" says the Bishop, "ocular demonstration! Well, I have preached, I have printed, upon the subject; but nothing will convince you sceptics but ocular demonstration. I am glad, Mr. Justice, you are become a convert. But pray, Sir, how went this affair? I beseech you, let me know the whole story." "My Lord, " answered the Justice, "as I lay one night in my bed, and had gone through the better half of my first sleep, it being about twelve o'clock, on a sudden I was awakened by a very strange and uncommon noise, and heard something coming up stairs, and stalking directly towards my room. I had the courage to raise myself upon my pillow, and to draw the curtain, just as I heard my chamber-door open, and saw a glimmering light enter my chamber." "Of a blue colour, no doubt, " says the Bishop. "Of a pale blue, " answers the Justice. "But, permit me, my good Lord, to proceed. The light was followed by a tall, meagre, and stern personage, who seemed to be of the age of seventy, in a long dangling rug gown, bound round his loins with a broad leathern girdle; his beard was thick and grizzly; he had a large fur cap on his head, and a long staff in his hand; his face was full of wrinkles, and seemed to be of a dark and sable hue. I was struck with the appearance of so surprising a figure, and felt some shocks which I had never before been acquainted with. Soon after the spectre had entered my room, with a hasty, but somewhat stately pace, it drew near my bed, and stared me full in the face." "And did you not speak to it?" interrupted the Bishop, with a good deal of emotion. "With submission, my Lord, " says the Justice, "please only to indulge me in a few words more." "But, Mr. Justice, Mr. Justice, " replies the Bishop still more hastily, "you should have spoken to it; there was money hid, or a murder committed; and give me leave to observe that murder is a matter cognizable by law, and this came regularly into judgment before you." "Well, my Lord, you will have your way; but, in short, I did speak to it." "And what answer, Mr. Justice, I pray you—what answer did it make you?" "My Lord, the answer was, not without a thump with the staff, and a shake of the lanthorn, that he was the watch-man of the night, and came to give me notice, that he had found the street-door open, and that, unless I arose and shut it, I might chance to be robbed before break of day."

The moment these words were out of the good Justice's mouth, the Bishop vanished with much more haste than did the supposed ghost, and in as great a surprise at the Justice's scepticism, as the Justice was at the Bishop's credulity.

THE
GHOSTLY ADVENTURER.

About thirty years ago, some labouring mechanics met one Saturday evening, after receiving their wages, at a public-house, near Rippon, in Yorkshire, for the purpose of enjoying themselves convivially, after the cares and fatigues of the week. The glass circulated freely: every man told his story, or sung a song; and various were the subjects of conversation. At length that of courage was introduced; every man now considered himself a hero, as is generally the case when liquor begins to operate. One boasted his skill as a pugilist, and related how many battles he had fought, and came off victorious; another related a dreadful encounter he had lately had with a mad dog, whom he overpowered and left dead on the field; a third told a story of his sleeping in a haunted house, and his conversation with a dreadful ghost. In short, various and extravagant were the different tales they told; until one, who had hitherto remained silent, arose, and told them that, notwithstanding their boasted courage, he would wager a bet of five guineas, that not one of the company had resolution sufficient to go to the bone-house, in the parish church-yard (which was about a mile distant), and bring a skull from thence with him, and place it on the table before the guests. This wager was soon accepted by one of the party, who immediately set off on his expedition to the church-yard. The wag who had proposed the bet, and who knew a nearer by-way to the bone-house than his opponent had taken, requested of the landlady to lend him a white sheet, and that he would soon cool this heroic man's courage. The landlady, who enjoyed the joke, complied with his request, lent him the sheet, and off set our wag with the utmost speed. He arrived at the bone-house first, threw the sheet over him, and placed himself in one corner, waiting the arrival of his comrade. Presently after enters the first man, with slow deliberate pace; and observing a figure in white, he felt himself greatly alarmed (as he afterwards acknowledged). However, he resumed his courage, advanced, stooped down, and picked up a skull. Immediately the phantom exclaimed, in a deep and hollow tone, "*That's my father's skull!*" "Well then, " replied the adventurer, "if it be thy father's skull, take it." So down he laid it, and took up another; when the figure replied, in the same hollow tone, "*That's my mother's skull!*" "Well then, " the other again replied, "if it be thy mother's skull, take it." So down he laid it, and took up a third. The apparition now, in a tremendously awful manner, cried out, "*That's my skull!*" "If it be the devil's skull, I'll have it!" answered the hero; and off he ran with it in his hand, greatly terrified, and the spectre after him.

In his flight through the church-yard, he stumbled over a tomb-stone, and fell; which occasioned the ghost likewise to fall upon him, which increased not a little his fright. However, he soon extricated himself, and again bent his flight towards the inn, which he soon reached; and, bolting suddenly into the room, exclaimed, with terrific countenance, his hair standing on end, "Here is the skull you sent me for: but, by George, the right owner's coming for it!" Saying which, down went the skull, and instantly appeared the figure with the white sheet on. This unexpected intrusion so much frightened all the company, that they ran out of the house as fast as possible, really believing it was an apparition from the tombs come to punish them for their sacrilegious theft. Such power has fear over the strongest mind when taken by surprise! The undaunted adventurer, however, won his wager; which was spent at the same house the Saturday following, when the joke was universally allowed to be a very good one.

THE
HEROIC MIDSHIPMAN;
OR
CHURCH-YARD ENCOUNTER.

At a respectable inn, in a market-town, in the west of England, some few years since, a regular set of the inhabitants met every evening to smoke their pipes, and pass a convivial hour. The conversation, as is usual at those places, was generally desultory. One evening, the subject introduced was concerning ghosts and apparitions; and many were the dreadful stories then told. A young midshipman, having accidentally dropped in, sat a silent and an attentive hearer; and, among other tales, heard a dreadful one of a sprite or hobgoblin dressed in white, which every night was seen hovering over the graves, in a church-yard at no great distance from the inn, and through which was a foot-path to one of the principal streets in the town. Our young gentleman felt himself stimulated with an ardour of quixotism at this relation; and was determined in his own mind, whatever might be the consequence, to encounter this nightly spectre, which so much disturbed the courageous inhabitants of the place. His pride was, to perform this mighty achievement alone. Therefore, between eleven and twelve o'clock at night, out he sallies, without making his intentions known to any one, and entered the church-yard. But, I should observe, that he had his hanger by his side. Having reached about the middle of the church-yard, he observed, sure enough, something in white moving backwards and forwards; but the haziness of the night prevented his strict discernment of the figure's shape. As it appeared advancing towards him, a momentary trepidation seized him. He retreated a few steps; but, soon recovering himself, he resolutely cried out, "*Who comes here?*" No answer being made, he again cried out, "*Who comes here?*" Still no reply was made. He then groped about for a stone or brick-bat, which having found, he threw with great violence at the figure; upon which it appeared to move much quicker than before. He again spoke to the figure; and, receiving no answer, drew his hanger, and made a desperate stroke at this dreadful spectre, which moving with still greater agility, now alarmed our adventurer, and caused him to run away greatly terrified, believing he had encountered some supernatural appearance, which had resisted all his blows. It was not long ere he reached home, and went to bed; but his fright was so great, that sleep could not gain any ascendancy over him. He therefore lay ruminating on this extraordinary affair the whole night. In the morning, while at breakfast, the bellman, or crier, came nearly under his window, and began his usual introductory address of "*O-yez! O-yez!*" These words immediately arrested the ears of our adventurer; and, to his very great astonishment, he heard him thus proceed—"This is to give notice, that whereas some evil-disposed person, or persons, did wantonly cut and maim the parson's white mare, which was grazing in the church-yard last night, a reward of ten guineas will be given to any person who will discover the offender, or offenders, so that they may be brought to justice! *God save the King!*" Our champion now thought it prudent to decamp without beat of drum. Thus ended this ghostly adventure; the particulars of which the inhabitants were informed of by letter, the moment the young gentleman had got safe on board his ship.

THE
COCK-LANE GHOST.

About the middle of January 1762, a gentleman was sent for to the house of one Parsons, the officiating parish clerk of St. Sepulchre's, in Cock Lane, near West Smithfield, to be witness to the noises, and other extraordinary circumstances, attending the supposed presence of a spirit, that, for two years preceding, had been heard in the night, to the great terror of the family. This knocking and scratching was always heard under the bed where the children lay; the eldest was about twelve years of age. To find out the cause, Mr. Parsons, the parish-clerk, ordered the wainscot to be taken down; which was accordingly done: but the noise, instead of ceasing, as he hoped, became more violent than ever. The children were afterwards removed into the two-pair of stairs room, where the same noise followed, and was frequently heard all night.

From these circumstances it was apprehended that the house was haunted; and the other child declared, that she, some time ago, had seen the apparition of a woman, surrounded, as it were, with a blazing light. About two years prior to which, a publican in the neighbourhood, bringing a pot of beer into the house, about eleven o'clock at night, was so frightened that he let the beer fall, upon seeing on the stairs, as he was looking up, a bright shining figure of a woman, by which he saw through a window into the charity-school, and saw the dial in the school. The figure passed by him, and beckoned him to follow; but he was too much terrified to obey its directions: he ran home, and was very sick. Soon after, Mr. Parsons himself, having occasion to go into another room, saw the same appearance. Both these happened within the space of an hour.

To throw some light upon this very mysterious affair, we shall begin with the narrative of Mr. Brown, of Amen Corner, published January 23d, 1762; the substance of which is as follows—

That in 1759, one Mr. K—— employed an agent to carry a letter to a young gentlewoman of a reputable family in Norfolk, and to bring her up to London in a post-chaise, if she would be willing to come. That she did come; but Mr. K—— being at Greenwich, she followed him there directly, and was received by him, after a journey of one hundred miles performed in one day, with much tenderness. After some short stay at Greenwich, where it was thought necessary that she should make a will in his favour, she was removed to a lodging near the Mansion-House; from thence to lodgings, behind St. Sepulchre's church; and, lastly, to a house in Bartlett Court, in the parish of Clerkenwell. Here, in 1760, she was taken ill of the small-pox; and, on or about the 31st of January, her sister, who lived reputably in Pall-Mall, was first made acquainted with her illness, and place of residence. Being greatly concerned thus to hear of her, she went immediately, and found her in a fair way of doing well; next day she sent, and received a favourable account of her; but, on the morning following, word was brought that her sister was dead. She died February 2d, 1760; and was buried, in two or three days after, at the church of St. John, Clerkenwell. Her sister, attending her funeral, was surprised at not seeing a plate upon the coffin, and expressed that surprise to Mr. Brown after the funeral was over; lamenting, at the same time, she had not been permitted to see her sister's corpse, the coffin being screwed down before she came. She added, that K—— had married one of her sisters, and had ruined the other, who was buried by the name of ——, as appears by the parish register. By the will already mentioned, K—— availed himself of her fortune, to the prejudice of her brother and sisters, who all lived in perfect harmony until this unhappy affair happened.

Such is the account given by Mr. Brown, of Amen Corner. A worthy clergyman, however, who attended her several times, and who administered to her the last comforts of his function, declares, that the small-pox with which she was seized, was of the confluent sort; and that the gentleman of the faculty, who attended her, had pronounced her irrecoverable some days before her death.

It was, however, the ghost of this person, that Parsons declared had taken possession of his girl, a child about twelve years old, who lay with the deceased in the absence of her supposed husband, when he was in the country at a wedding; and then it was, that the knocking was first heard, to the great terror of this child, she frequently crying out that she might not be taken away. Soon after, this woman died, whose apparition was now supposed to appear to this same child; and, in answer to the question put to her, What was the occasion of the first knocking, &c. before she died? answered, that it was the spirit of her sister, the first wife of Mr. K——, who was husband to them both.

Having now sufficiently prepared the reader, we shall proceed in our narrative. The gentleman already said to have been sent for, attended, and found the child in bed; and, the spirit being at hand, several questions were put to it by the father, which, to avoid repetition, we shall relate hereafter. The gentleman not caring to pronounce too hastily upon what appeared to him extraordinary, got some friends together, among whom were two or three clergymen, about twenty other persons, and two negroes, who sat up another night.

They first thoroughly examined the bed, bed-clothes, &c.;

and, being satisfied that there was no visible appearance of deceit, the child with its sister was put into bed, which was found to shake extremely by the gentleman who had placed himself at the foot of it. Among others, the following questions were asked—

Whether her disturbance was occasioned by any ill-treatment from Mr. K——?—Yes.

Whether she was brought to an untimely end by poison?—Yes.

In what was the poison administered, beer or purl?—Purl.

How long before her death?—Three hours.

Is the person called Carrots, able to give information about the poison?—Yes.

Whether she was K——'s wife's sister?—Yes.

Whether she was married to K——?—No.

Whether any other person than K—— was concerned in the poisoning?—No.

Whether she could visibly appear to any one?—Yes.

Whether she would do so?—Yes.

Whether she could go out of that house?—Yes.

Whether she would follow the child everywhere?—Yes.

Whether she was pleased at being asked questions?—Yes.

Whether it eased her mind?—Yes. (Here a mysterious noise, compared to the fluttering of wings round the room, was heard.)

How long before her death had she told Carrots (her servant) that she was poisoned?—One hour. (Here Carrots, who was admitted to be one of the company on Tuesday night, asserted that the deceased had not told her so, she being at that time speechless.)

How long did Carrots live with her?—Three or four days. (Carrots attested the truth of this.)

Whether, if the accused should be taken up, he would confess?—Yes.

Whether she should be at ease in her mind, if the man was hanged?—Yes.

How long it would be before he would be executed?—Three years.

How many clergymen were in the room?—Three.

How many negroes?—Two.

Whether she could distinguish the person of any one in the room?—Yes.

Whether the colour of a watch held up by one of the clergymen was white, yellow, blue, or black?—Black. (The watch was in a black shagreen case.)

At what time she would depart in the morning?—At four o'clock.

Accordingly, at this hour the noise removed to the Wheat-sheaf, a public-house at the distance of a few doors, in the bed-chamber of the landlord and landlady, to the great affright and terror of them both. Such was the manner of interrogating the spirit: the answer was given by knocking or scratching. An affirmative was one knock; a negative, two. Displeasure was expressed by scratching.

Nothing more occurred till the following morning, when the knocking began about seven o'clock. But, notwithstanding some extraordinary answers to the several questions proposed, it was still a matter of doubt whether the whole was not a piece of imposition; and it was resolved to remove the child elsewhere. Accordingly, instead of its being carried home, it was conveyed to a house in Crown-and-Cushion Court, at the upper end of Cow Lane, near Smithfield, where two clergymen, several gentlemen, and some ladies, assembled in the evening.

About eleven o'clock the knocking began; when a gentleman in the room, speaking angrily to the girl, and hinting that he suspected it was some trick of her's, the child was uneasy, and cried: on which the knocking was heard louder, and much faster than before; but no answer could be obtained to any question while that gentleman staid in the room.

After he was gone, the noise ceased: and nothing was heard

till a little after twelve o'clock, when the child was seized with a trembling and shivering; in which manner she had always been affected, on the departure as well as the approach of the ghost. Upon this, one of the company asked, whether it would return again, and at what time? Answer was made in the usual manner by knocks, that it would return again before seven in the morning; and then a noise, like the fluttering of wings, was heard; after which all was quiet till between six and seven on Friday morning, when the knocking began again.

A little before seven, two clergymen came, when the fluttering noise was repeated, which in this strange affair was considered as a mark of the spirit's being pleased. Then several questions, particularly one, by a gentlewoman who was an acquaintance of the deceased, who came out of mere curiosity, and had been to see her some time before she died: the question was, How many days it was before her death, that this gentlewoman came to see her? The answer given was three knocks, signifying three days; which was exactly right. Another question was, Whether some of the then company had not a relation that had been buried in the same vault where she lay? To which it replied by one knock, Yes. They asked, severally, if it was their relation? To all of which, except the last, she answered by two knocks, meaning No; but to the last person she gave one knock, which was right. These two circumstances greatly alarmed all the company.

Near twenty persons sat up in the room: but it was not till about six o'clock in the morning that the first alarm was given, which coming spontaneously, as well as suddenly, a good deal struck the imagination of the auditors. The scratches were compared to that of a cat upon a cane chair. The child now appeared to be in a sound sleep, and nothing further could be obtained. It had been observed, in conversation, by a person who expressed himself pretty warmly on the subject, that the whole was an imposture, and more to the same purpose; which gave rise to some sharp altercation among the company—some believing, and others disbelieving the reality of the apparition. This dispute was no sooner begun, than the spirit was gone; and no more knocking and scratching was to be heard.

About seven o'clock the girl seemed to awake in a violent fit of crying and tears. Upon being asked the occasion, and assured that nothing of harm should happen to her, she declared that her tears were the effect of her imagination at what would become of her daddy, who must needs be ruined and undone, if this matter should be supposed to be an imposture. She was told, that the company had looked upon her as in a sound sleep when the above dispute happened. To which she replied, "Aye, but not so sound but that I could hear all you said."

On the Sunday night following, the girl lay at a house opposite the school-house in Cock Lane; at which place a person of distinction, two clergymen, and several other persons, were present. Between ten and eleven o'clock the knocking began: the principal questions and answers were the same as those already mentioned; but among some new ones of little consequence, was the following?—Will you attend the girl at any place whither she may be appointed to be carried, by authority? Answered in the affirmative. At eleven o'clock, eleven distinct knocks were heard; and at twelve, when being asked if it was going away, and when it would return again, seven knocks were given. Accordingly, when St. Sepulchre's clock struck seven, on Monday morning, this invisible agent knocked the same number of times. Some few questions were asked at this meeting, much to the same purport as those above inserted, and answered in the same manner. Every person was put out of the room, who could be supposed to have the least connexion with the girl: her hands were laid over the bed-clothes, and the bed narrowly looked under, &c. but no discovery was made.

On the night of the 1st of February, many gentlemen, eminent for their rank and character, were, by the invitation of the Reverend Mr. Aldrich, of Clerkenwell, assembled at his house, for the examination of the noises supposed to be made by a departed spirit for the detection of some enormous crime.

About ten at night, the gentlemen met in the chamber, in which the girl supposed to be disturbed by a spirit had, with proper caution, been put to bed by several ladies. They sat with her rather more than an hour; and, hearing nothing, went down stairs, when they interrogated the father of the girl, who denied, in the strongest terms, any knowledge or belief of fraud.

The supposed spirit had before publicly promised, by an affirmative knock, that it would attend one of the gentlemen into the vault under the church of St. John, Clerkenwell, where the body was deposited; and give a token of her presence there, by a knock upon her coffin: it was, therefore, determined to make this trial of the existence or veracity of the supposed spirit.

While they were inquiring and deliberating, they were summoned into the girl's chamber by the ladies who remained near her bed, and who heard knocks and scratches. When the gentlemen entered, the girl declared that she felt the spirit like a mouse upon her back, and was required to hold her hands out of bed. From that time, though the spirit was very solemnly required to manifest its existence, by appearance, by impression on the hand or body of any person present, by scratches, knocks, or any other agency, no evidence of any preternatural power was exhibited.

The spirit was then very seriously advertised, that the person to whom the promise was made, of striking the coffin, was then about to visit the vault, and that the performance of the promise was then claimed. The company, at one o'clock, went into the church; and that gentleman, to whom the promise was made, went, with one more, into the vault. The spirit was very solemnly required to perform its promise, but nothing more than silence ensued: the person supposed to be accused by the spirit then went down, with several others, but no effect was perceived. Upon their return, they examined the girl, but could draw no confession from her. Between two and three, she desired, and was permitted, to go home with her father.

No doubt now remained of the fallacy of this spirit. It was supposed that the girl was practised in the art of ventriloquism, an art better known now than formerly; but it was soon after discovered that there was not so much ingenuity in the fraud.

A bed was slung like a hammock, in the middle of a room, at a gentleman's house, where the girl was sent. The servants were ordered to watch her narrowly; and, about a quarter of an hour before bed-time, she was observed to conceal something under her clothes. Information of this being given to the gentlemen attending, they were of opinion, that a connivance at the beginning of the scene would be the most likely means of leading them to a full discovery of the fact. In the morning, about six o'clock, the knockings came, and answered to questions as usual, but in so different a sound, that it was very apparent this method of operating was a fresh contrivance. When the knockings, which continued for near half an hour, were over, she was several times asked, if she had any wood or other thing in the bed, against which she could strike? which she obstinately denied. Two maid-servants being then ordered to take her out of bed, a piece of board was found in it, which, as was observed, she had conveyed there the night before.

Soon after, a trial came on before Lord Mansfield, in the Court of King's Bench, Guildhall, by a special jury, on an indictment against Richard Parsons, and Elizabeth his wife, Mary Fraser, a clergyman, and a reputable tradesman, for a conspiracy in the Cock-Lane ghost affair, to injure the character, &c. of Mr. William Kent; when they were all found guilty. The trial lasted about twelve hours.

THE
HYPOCHONDRIAC GENTLEMAN
AND THE JACK-ASS.

A sober gentleman of very great respectability, who was low-spirited and hypochondriac to a degree, was at times so fanciful, that almost every rustling noise he heard was taken for an apparition or hobgoblin.

It happened that he was abroad at a friend's house later than ordinary one night; but, it being moon-light, and having a servant with him, he seemed to be easy, and was observed to be cheerful, and even merry, with a great deal more of good-humour than had been observed in him for some time before.

He knew his way perfectly well, for it was within three miles of the town where he lived, and he was very well mounted: but, though the moon was up, an accident, which a little disordered him, was, that a very thick black cloud appeared to him to come suddenly over his head, which made it very dark; and, to add to his discomfort, it began to rain violently.

Upon this he resolved to ride for it, having not above two miles to the town; so, clapping spurs to his horse, he galloped away. His man (whose name was Jervais), not being so well mounted, was a considerable way behind. The darkness of the night, and the rain together, put him a little out of humour, and made him ride rather harder than his usual pace.

In his way home, there was a small river for him to pass; but there was a good bridge over it, well walled on both sides, so that there was no more danger than in any other place. The gentleman kept on at a good pace, and was rather more than half over the bridge, when his horse stopped all on a sudden, and would not go on. He saw nothing at first, and was therefore not much discomposed at it, but spurred his horse to go forward. The horse then went two or three steps; then stopped again, snorted, and started; then attempted to turn short back. The gentleman, in endeavouring to see what frightened the horse, saw two broad staring eyes looking him full in the face.

He was now most heartily frightened; but, by this time, he heard his man Jervais coming up. When he came near, the first thing he heard his master say, was, "Bless me, it is the devil!" at which exclamation the man was almost as much frightened as his master. However, the gentleman, a little encouraged to hear his man so near him, pressed his horse once more to go forward, and called aloud to his servant to follow; but Jervais, being much frightened, made no haste. At length, with great difficulty, he got over the bridge, and passed by the creature with the broad staring eyes, which he positively affirmed was the devil.

Though Jervais was near enough, yet fearing his master would order him to go before, he kept as far off as he possibly could. When his master called, he answered, but proceeded very slowly, till he observed his master had gone past; when, being obliged to follow, he went on very softly till he came to the bridge, where he plainly saw what it was his master's horse snorted at, which the reader will be made acquainted with presently.

The gentleman, having now past the difficulty, galloped home as fast as possible, and got into the house long before Jervais could get up with him. As soon as he alighted, he swooned away, such an effect the fright had on him; and with much difficulty they brought him to himself. When he recovered, he told the family a formal story, that at such a bridge he met with the devil, who was standing at the left-hand corner of the wall, and stared him full in the face; and he so fully expatiated on this subject, that all believed, at least, he had met with an apparition.

Jervais soon after came home, and went directly to the stable to take care of the horses; where he told *his story* in the following manner to his fellow-servants: "Finding, " says he, "that my master was in danger of being thrown over the bridge, I fearlessly rode near him; when, to my very great surprise, I found that my master's horse (which was young and skittish) was frightened at an ass, which stood grazing near the corner of the wall." "Are you sure it was an ass, Jervais?" asked the servants, staring one at another, half frightened themselves. "Are you quite sure of it?" "Yes, " replied the man; "for, as soon as my master had got by, I rode up to it; and, on discovering the cause of our fear, I thrashed it with my stick, on which it fell a braying; and I rode home after my master." "Why, Jervais, " said the servants, "your master believes it was the devil." "I am sorry, " said the man, "my master should have been so much deceived; but, really, it was nothing more nor less than an ass."

The story now got vent; and the first part of it flew all over the town, that Mr. —— (mentioning his name) had seen the devil, and was almost frightened to death.

Shortly after, the man's tale was circulated, that Mr. ——'s strange and wonderful apparition of the devil was nothing more than an ass; which raised the laugh sufficiently against the master.

However, poor Jervais lost his place for gossiping; and his master insists upon it to this day, that it was the devil, and that he knew him by his broad eyes and cloven feet. Such is the power of imagination over the weak and credulous!

THE
CASTLE APPARITION.

Translated by the Rev. Weeden Butler,
Jun. from a Monkish Manuscript.

In the vicinity of Chamberry, a town in Savoy, stood the ancient mansion of the Albertini: round it were several little buildings, in which were deposited the cattle, poultry, &c. &c. belonging to the family. A young gentleman, by name Barbarosse, came to the chateau on a visit for a few days; he was cordially received, being of a pleasing lively disposition; and an elegant room in the east wing was prepared for his accommodation.

The family, and their young guests, spent the day very agreeably; and, after supper, they sat round a comfortable large fire, and diverted themselves with songs and stories: the former, as is generally the case, were some of the sprightly, some of the tender and pathetic kind; but the latter were, for the most part, of the melancholy cast, particularly those which related to preternatural occurrences. The social party separated at half past twelve o'clock; and Barbarosse retired to his chamber. It was a handsome room on the first floor, having three doors; two of these belonged to two little closets, one on the right that overlooked a farm-yard, and another more to the left that presented a view through the window of a large romantic wood; the third door was that by which he entered his room, after traversing a long passage. Our youth had visited this room in the morning, and looked out of the window to enjoy the prospect for a great while.

As he entered this apartment, with his mind full of the diversion just left, he set his candle down upon the table, and looked about him. There was an excellent fire in the chimney, with an iron grating before it, to prevent accidents; a large elbow-chair stood near it; and, not being at all sleepy, he sat down reflecting on the amusements of the day, and endeavoured to remember the tales he had heard. In some he thought he perceived strong traits of truth; and in others he discovered palpable fiction and absurdity. Whilst he was deliberating on the various incidents, the heavy watch-bell tolled two; but Barbarosse did not attend to it, being deeply engaged in his contemplations. He was suddenly awakened from his reveries by an uncommon rustling sound issuing from the closet on the right hand; and, listening attentively, he heard distinct taps upon the floor at short intervals.

Alarmed at the circumstance, he walked slowly to his bed-side, and drew forth his pocket-pistols from under the pillow; these he carefully placed upon the table, and resumed the elbow-chair. All was again still as death; and nought but the winds, which whistled round the watch-tower and the adjacent buildings, could be heard.

Barbarosse looked towards the door of the closet, which he then, and not till then, perceived was not shut, but found that it hung upon the jar; immediately a furious blast forced it wide open; the taper burnt blue, and the fire seemed almost extinct.

Barbarosse arose, put forth a silent hasty ejaculation of prayer, and sat down again; again he heard the noise! He started up, seized the pistols, and stood motionless; whilst large cold drops of dew hung upon his face. Still his heart continued firm, and he grew more composed, when the rustling taps were renewed! Barbarosse desperately invoked the protection of Heaven, cocked one of the pistols, and was about to rush into the portentous apartment, when the noise increased and drew nearer: a loud peal of thunder, that seemed to rend the firmament, shook violently the solid battlements of the watch-tower; the deep-toned bell tolled three, and its hollow sound long vibrated on the ear of Barbarosse with fainter and fainter murmurs; when a tremendous cry thrilled him with terror and dismay; and, lo! the long-dreaded spectre stalked into the middle of the room: and Barbarosse, overcome with surprise and astonishment at the *unexpected* apparition, sunk down *convulsed*[B] in his chair.

The phantom was armed *de cap en pied*, and clad in a black garment. On his crest a black plume waved majestically; and, instead of a glove or any other sort of lady's favour, he wore a blood-red token. He bore no weapon of offence in his hand; but a gloomy shield, made of the feathers of some kind of bird, was cast over each shoulder. He was booted and spurred; and, looking upon Barbarosse with ardent eyes, raised his feathery arms, and struck them vehemently against his sides, making at the same time the most vociferous noise!

Then it was, that Barbarosse found he had not shut down the window in the morning; from which neglect it happened, that a *black game-cock* had flown into the closet, and created all this inexpressible confusion.

FOOTNOTES:

[B]Lest any of the faculty should wish, ineffectually, to be informed what species of convulsions affected Barbarosse, I think it proper (observes the translator) to satisfy their truly laudable curiosity by anticipation, and to assure them, *fois d'homme d'honneur*, that this disorder was a *convulsion of laughter*.

THE TWINS,
OR
GHOST OF THE FIELD.

———————————

Ye who delight in old traditions,
And love to talk of apparitions,
Whose chairs around are closely join'd,
While no one dares to look behind,
Thinking there's some hobgoblin near,
Ready to whisper in his ear;
Oh! listen, while I lay before ye
My well-authenticated story.

Two twins, of understanding good,
Together liv'd, as brothers should:
This was named Thomas, that was John;
But all things else they had as one.
At length, by industry in trade,
They had a pretty fortune made,
And had, like others in the city,
A country cottage very pretty;
Where they amused their leisure hours,
In innocence, with plants and flowers,
Till fate had cut Tom's thread across,
And left poor John to wail his loss.

John left alone, when now some weeks
Had wip'd the tears from off his cheeks,
To muse within himself began
On what should be his future plan:

"Ye woods, ye fields, my sweet domain,
When shall I see your face again?
When shall I pass the vacant hours,
Rejoicing in my woodbine bowers;
To smoke my pipe, and sing my song;
Regardless how they pass along?
When take my fill of pastime there,
In sweet forgetfulness of care?"

He said; and, on his purpose bent,
Soon to his country cottage went,
Swill'd home-brew'd ale and gooseberry fool:
John never ate or drank by rule.

His arms were folded now to rest,
The night-mare sat upon his breast;
From right to left, and left to right,
He turn'd and toss'd, throughout the night:
A thousand fears disturb'd his head,
And phantoms danced around his bed;
His lab'ring stomach, though he slept,
The fancy wide awake had kept:
His brother's ghost approach'd his side,
And thus in feeble accents cried—
"Be not alarm'd, my brother dear,
To see your buried partner here;
I come to tell you where to find
A treasure, which I left behind:
I had not time to let you know it,
But follow me, and now I'll shew it."
John trembled at the awful sight,
But hopes of gain suppress'd his fright;
Oft will the parching thirst of gold,
Make even errant cowards bold.

John, rising up without delay,
Went where the spectre led the way;
Which, after many turnings past,
Stopp'd in an open field at last,
Where late the hind had sow'd his grain,
And made the whole a level plain.
The spectre pointed to the spot,
Where he had hid the golden pot:
"Deep in the earth," says he, "'tis laid."
But John, alas! had got no spade;
And, as the night was pretty dark,
He felt around him for a mark,
That he might know again the place,
Soon as Aurora shew'd her face.
In vain he stoop'd and felt around,
No stick or stone was to be found;
But nature now, before oppress'd,
By change of posture sore distress'd,
Gave an alarming crack; a hint
Of what, as sure as stick or flint,
To-morrow morn the place would tell,
If he had either sight or smell.
This done, he rose to go to bed;
He wak'd, how chang'd! the night-mare fled;
The ghost was vanish'd from his sight,
And John himself in piteous plight.

THE
DOUBLE MISTAKE,
OR
COLLEGE GHOST.

Mr. Samuel Foote, the celebrated comedian, played the following trick upon Doctor Gower, who was then provost of his college, a man of considerable learning, but rather of a grave pedantic turn of mind.

The church belonging to the college fronted the side of a lane, where cattle were sometimes turned out to graze during the night; and from the steeple hung the bell-rope, very low in the middle of the outside porch. Foote saw in this an object likely to produce some fun, and immediately set about to accomplish his purpose. He accordingly, one night, slily tied a wisp of hay to the rope, as a bait for the cows in their peregrination to the grazing ground. The scheme succeeded to his wish. One of the cows soon after, smelling the hay as she passed by the church-door, instantly seized on it, and, by tugging at the rope, made the bell ring, to the astonishment of the sexton and the whole parish.

This happened several nights successively; and the incident gave rise to various reports—such as, not only that the church was haunted by evil spirits, but that several spectres were seen walking about the church-yard, in all those hideous and frightful shapes, which fear, ignorance, and fancy, usually suggest on such occasions.

An event of this kind, however, was to be explored, for the honour of philosophy, as well as for the quiet of the parish. Accordingly, the Doctor and the sexton agreed to sit up one night, and, on the first alarm, to run out, and drag the culprit to condign punishment. Their plan being arranged, they waited with the utmost impatience for the appointed signal: at last, the bell began to sound its usual alarm, and they both sallied out in the dark, determined on making a discovery.

The sexton was the first in the attack: he seized the cow by the tail, and cried out it was a gentleman commoner, as he had him by the tail of his gown; while the Doctor, who had caught the cow by the horns at the same time, immediately replied, "No, no, you blockhead, 'tis the postman; and here I have hold of the rascal by his blowing-horn." Lights however were immediately brought, when the character of the real offender was discovered, and the laugh of the whole town was turned upon the Doctor.

THE
HAUNTED CASTLE.

The castle of Ardivillers, near Breteuil, was reported to be haunted by evil spirits. Dreadful noises were heard; and flames were seen, by night, to issue from various apertures. The farmer who was entrusted with the care of the house, in the absence of its owner, the President d'Ardivillers, could alone live there. The spirit seemed to respect him; but any person who ventured to take up a night's lodging in the castle was sure to bear the marks of his audacity.

Superstition is catching. The peasants in the neighbourhood at length began to see strange sights. Sometimes a dozen of ghosts would appear in the air above the castle dancing. At other times, a number of presidents and counsellors, in red robes, appeared in the adjacent meadow. There they sat in judgment on a gentleman of the country, who had been beheaded for some crime an hundred years before. In short, many had seen, and all had heard, the wonders of the castle of Ardivillers.

This affair had continued four or five years, to the great loss of the President, who had been obliged to let the estate to the farmer at a very low rent. At length, suspecting some artifice, he resolved to visit and inspect the castle himself.

Taking with him two gentlemen, his friends, they determined to pass the night in the same apartment; and if any noise or apparition disturbed them, to discharge their pistols at either ghost or sound. As spirits know all things, they were probably aware of these preparations, and not one appeared. But, in the chamber just above, a dreadful rattling of chains was heard; and the wife and children of the farmer ran to assist their lord. They threw themselves on their knees, begging that he would not visit that terrible room. "My lord, " said they, "what can human force effect against people of t'other world? Monsieur de Ficancout attempted the same enterprise years ago, and he returned with a dislocated arm. M. D'Urselles tried too; he was overwhelmed with bundles of hay, and was ill for a long time after." In short, so many attempts were mentioned, that the President's friends advised *him* to abandon the design.

But still *they* determined to encounter the danger. Proceeding up stairs to an extensive room, each having a candle in one hand, and a pistol in the other, they found it full of thick smoke, which increased more and more from some flames that were visible. Soon after, the ghost or spirit faintly appeared in the middle: he seemed quite black, and was amusing himself with cutting capers; but another eruption of flame and smoke hid him from their view. He had horns and a long tail; and was, in truth, a dreadful object.

One of the gentlemen found his courage rather fail. "This is certainly supernatural, " said he; "let us retire." The other, endued with more boldness, asserted that the smoke was that of gunpowder, which is no supernatural composition; "and if this same spirit, " added he, "knew his own nature and trade, he should have extinguished our candles."

With these words, he jumped amidst the smoke and flames, and pursued the spectre. He soon discharged the pistol at his back, and hit him exactly in the middle; but was himself seized with fear, when the spirit, far from falling, turned round and rushed upon him. Soon recovering himself, he resolved to grasp the ghost, to discover if it were indeed aërial and impassable. Mr. Spectre, disordered by this new manœuvre, rushed to the tower, and descended a small staircase.

The gentleman ran after, and, never losing sight of him, passed several courts and gardens, still turning as the spirit winded, till at length they entered into an open barn. Here the pursuer, certain, as he thought, of his prey, shut the door, but when he turned round, what was his amazement, to see the spirit totally disappear.

In great confusion, he called to the servants for more lights. On examining the spot of the spirit's disappearance, he found a trap-door; upon raising which, several mattresses appeared, to break the fall of any headlong adventurer. Therefore, descending, he found the spirit to be no other than the *farmer* himself. His dress, of a complete bull's hide, had secured him from the pistol-shot; and the horns and tail were not diabolic, but mere natural appendages of the original. The rogue confessed his tricks, and was pardoned, on paying the arrears due for five years, at the old rent of the land.

THE
HAMMERSMITH GHOST.

In the year 1804, the inhabitants of Hammersmith were much alarmed by a nocturnal appearance; which, for a considerable time, eluded detection or discovery. In the course of this unfortunate affair, two innocent persons met with an untimely death; and as this transaction engaged the attention of the public in a high degree, we shall fully relate the particulars of it.

An unknown person made it his diversion to alarm the inhabitants, in January 1804, by assuming the figure of a spectre. This sham ghost has certainly much to answer for. One poor woman, who was far advanced in her pregnancy of a second child, was so much shocked, that she took to her bed, and survived only two days. She had been crossing near the church-yard about ten o'clock at night, when she beheld something, as she described, rise from the tomb-stones. The figure was very tall, and very white! She attempted to run, but the supposed ghost soon overtook her, and, pressing her in his arms, she fainted; in which situation she remained some hours, till discovered by the neighbours, who kindly led her home, when she took to her bed, from which, alas! she never rose. A waggoner belonging to Mr. Russell was also so alarmed, while driving a team of eight horses, which had sixteen passengers at the time, that he took to his heels, and left the waggon, horses, and passengers, in the greatest danger. Neither man, woman, or child, would pass that way for some time; and the report was, that it was the apparition of a man who had cut his throat in that neighbourhood above a year before. Several lay in wait different nights for the ghost; but there were so many bye-lanes, and paths leading to Hammersmith, that he was always sure of being in that which was unguarded, and every night played off his tricks, to the terror of the passengers.

One Francis Smith, doubtless incensed at the unknown person who was in the habit of assuming the supernatural character, and thus frightening the superstitious inhabitants of the village, rashly determined on watching for, and shooting the ghost; when, unfortunately, in Black-Lion Lane, he shot a poor innocent man, Thomas Millwood, a bricklayer, who was in a white dress, the usual habiliment of his occupation. This rash act, having been judged wilful murder by the coroner's inquest, Smith was accordingly committed to gaol, and took his trial at the ensuing sessions at the Old Bailey, January 13th, 1804. The jury at first found him guilty of manslaughter; but the crime being deemed murder in the eye of the law, the judge could only receive a verdict of Guilty, or acquittal. He was then found guilty, and received sentence of death, but was afterwards pardoned on condition of being imprisoned one year.

THE
FRIGHTENED CARRIER.

In October 1813, a little before midnight, as one of the carriers between Nottingham and Loughborough, was passing near the village of Rempstone, he was extremely surprised at meeting what he thought was a funeral procession, marching in a most solemn and steady order in the centre of the road. The carrier, with a becoming propriety and decorum, drew his cart to the side of the road, that the mournful cavalcade might pass without any interruption. Very active inquiry was immediately afterwards made in the neighbourhood, but not the least knowledge could be obtained as to where this solemn group had come from, or whither it was going; it was therefore concluded, that some ghostly apparition or other had thought proper to be then exercising its nocturnal avocation. Some days afterwards it was found out, that a person, who lived in the neighbouring village, had been endeavouring to construct a carriage upon such a principle as to go without horses; and, wishing to make his experiment as secret as possible, had chosen that dead hour of the night, for trying his apparatus on the turnpike road; but unluckily meeting with the carrier, he became alarmed for fear of an exposure, and therefore threw a large sheet over the machinery, and passed the cart as silently as possible, to avoid being detected.

THE
CLUB-ROOM GHOST.

At a town in the west of England, was held a club of twenty-four persons, which assembled once a week, to drink punch, smoke tobacco, and talk politics. Like Rubens's Academy at Antwerp, each member had his peculiar chair, and the president's was more exalted than the rest. One of the members had been in a dying state for some time; of course, his chair, while he was absent, remained vacant.

The club being met on their usual night, inquiries were naturally made after their associate. As he lived in the adjoining house, a particular friend went himself to inquire for him, and returned with the dismal tidings, that he could not possibly survive the night. This threw a gloom on the company, and all efforts to turn the conversation from the sad subject before them were ineffectual.

About midnight (the time, by long prescription, appropriated for the walking of spectres), the door opened; and the form, in white, of the dying, or rather of the dead man, walked into the room, and took his seat in the accustomed chair: there he remained in silence, and in silence was he gazed at. The apparition continued a sufficient time in the chair to convince all present of the reality of the vision: at length, he arose, and stalked towards the door, which he opened as if living—went out, and then shut the door after him. After a long pause, some one, at last, had the resolution to say, "If only one of us had seen this, he would not have been believed; but it is impossible that so many persons can be deceived."

The company, by degrees, recovered their speech; and the whole conversation, as may be imagined, was upon the dreadful object which had engaged their attention. They broke up, and went home. In the morning, inquiry was made after their sick friend; it was answered by an account of his death, which happened nearly at the time of his appearing in the club. There could be little doubt before, but now nothing could be more certain, than the reality of the apparition, which had been seen by so many persons together.

It is needless to say, that such a story spread over the country, and found credit, even from infidels; for, in this case, all reasoning became superfluous, when opposed to a plain fact, attested by three-and-twenty witnesses. To assert the doctrine of the fixed laws of nature, was ridiculous, when there were so many people of credit to prove that they might be unfixed. Years rolled on; the story ceased to engage attention, and it was forgotten, unless when occasionally produced to silence an unbeliever.

One of the club was an apothecary. In the course of his

practice, he was called to an old woman, whose profession was attending on sick persons. She told him, that she could leave the world with a quiet conscience, but for one thing which lay on her mind. "Do not you remember Mr. ——, whose ghost has been so much talked of? I was his nurse. The night he died, I left the room for something that was wanted. I am sure I had not been absent long; but, at my return, I found the bed without my patient. He was delirious; and I feared that he had thrown himself out of the window. I was so frightened that I had no power to stir; but, after some time, to my great astonishment, he entered the room shivering, and his teeth chattering—laid down on the bed, and died. Considering myself as the cause of his death, I kept this a secret, for fear of what might be done to me. Though I could contradict all the story of the ghost, I dared not do it. I knew, by what had happened, that it was he himself who had been in the club-room (perhaps recollecting, in his delirium, that it was the night of meeting): but I hope God and the poor gentleman's friends will forgive me, and then I shall die contented."

THE
LUNATIC APPARITION.

The celebrated historian De Thou had a very singular adventure at Saumer, in the year 1598. One night, having retired to rest, very much fatigued, while he was enjoying a sound sleep, he felt a very extraordinary weight upon his feet, which, having made him turn suddenly, fell down and awakened him. At first he imagined that it had been only a dream: but, hearing soon after some noise in the chamber, he drew aside the curtains, and saw, by the help of the moon (which at that time shone very bright), a large white figure walking up and down; and, at the same time, observed upon a chair some rags, which he thought belonged to thieves who had come to rob him. The figure then approaching his bed, he had the courage to ask it what it was. "I am, " said it, "the *Queen of Heaven.*" Had such a figure appeared to any credulous ignorant man in the dead of night, and made such a speech, would he not have trembled with fear, and have frightened the whole neighbourhood with a marvellous description of it? But De Thou had too much understanding to be so imposed upon. Upon hearing the words which dropped from the figure, he immediately concluded that it was some mad woman, got up, called his servants, and ordered them to turn her out of doors; after which he returned to bed, and fell asleep. Next morning he found that he had not been deceived in his conjecture; and that, having forgot to shut his door, this female figure had escaped from her keepers, and entered his apartment. The brave Schomberg, to whom De Thou related this adventure, some days after, confessed, that in such a case he should not have shewn so much courage. The King also, who was informed of it by Schomberg, made the same acknowledgment.

SUPPOSED SUPERNATURAL APPEARANCE.

Some few years since, before ghosts and spectres were commonly introduced among us by means of the pantomimes and novels of the day, a gentleman of a philosophical turn of mind, who was hardy enough to deny the existence of any thing supernatural, happened to pay a visit at an old house in Gloucestershire, whose unfortunate owner had just become a bankrupt, with a view to offer such assistance and consolation as he could bestow: when, in one rainy dull evening in the month of March, the family being seated by the kitchen fireside, the conversation turned on supernatural appearances. The philosopher was endeavouring to convince his auditors of the folly and absurdity of such opinions, with rather an unbecoming levity, when the wife left the party and went up stairs; but had hardly quitted the kitchen three minutes, before a dreadful noise was heard, mingled with horrid screams. The poor maid changed countenance, and her red hair stood erect, in every direction; the husband trembled in his chair; and the philosopher began to look serious. At last, the husband rose from his seat, and ascended the stairs in search of his wife, when a second dreadful scream was heard: the maid mustered resolution to follow her master, and a third scream ensued. The philosopher, who was not quite at ease, now thought it high time for him to set out in search of a *cause*: when, arriving at the landing-place, he found the maid in a fit; the master lying flat, with his face upon the floor, which was stained with blood; and, on advancing a little farther, the mistress in nearly the same condition. To the latter the philosopher paid immediate attention; and, finding she had only swooned away, brought her in his arms down stairs, and placed her on the floor of the kitchen. The pump was at hand, and he had the presence of mind to run to it to get some water in a glass; but what was his astonishment, when he found that he pumped only copious streams of blood! which extraordinary appearance, joined to the other circumstances, made the unbeliever tremble in every limb: a sudden perspiration overspread the surface of his skin; and the supernatural possessed his imagination in all its true colours of dread and horror. Again and again he repeated his efforts; and, again and again, threw away the loathsome contents of the glass.

Had the story stopped here, what would not superstition have made of it? But the philosopher, who was still pumping, now found the water grew paler; and, at last, pure water filled the vessel. Overjoyed at this observation, he threw the limpid stream in the face of the mistress, whose recovery was assisted by the appearance of her husband and Betty.

The mystery, when explained, turned out to be simply this— The good housewife, when she knew that a docket had been struck against her husband, had taken care to conceal some of her choice cherry brandy, from the rapacious gripe of the messenger to the Commissioners of Bankrupts, on some shelves in a closet up stairs, which also contained, agreeably to the ancient architecture of the building, the trunk of the pump below; and, in trying to move the jars, to get at a drop for the party at the kitchen fire, the shelf gave way with a tremendous crash; the jars were broken into an hundred pieces; the rich juice descended in torrents down the trunk of the pump, and filled, with its ruby current, the sucker beneath; and this was the self-same fluid which the philosopher, in his fright, had so madly thrown away. The wife had swooned at the accident; the husband, in his haste, had fallen on his nose, which ran with blood; and the maid's legs, in her hurry, coming in contact with her fallen master's ribs, she, like "vaulting ambition, " overleaped herself, and fell on the other side.

Often has this story been told, by one who knew the philosopher, with great effect, till the last act, or *denouement*; when disappointment was mostly visible in the looks of his auditors, at finding there was actually nothing supernatural in the affair, and no ghost.

THE
APPARITION INVESTIGATED.

In a village in one of the midland counties of Scotland, lived a widow, distinguished among her neighbours for decency of manners, integrity, and respect for religion. She affirmed that, for several nights together, she had heard a supernatural voice exclaiming aloud, *Murder! Murder!* This was immediately reported through the neighbourhood: all were alarmed, and looked around them with solicitude for the detection of the murder which they supposed to have been committed; and it was not long till a discovery seemed actually to be made. It was reported, that a gentleman, who had relations at no great distance, and had been residing in the West Indies, had lately arrived with a considerable fortune; that he had lodged at an inn about three miles off; and that he had afterwards been seen entering a house in the village where the widow lived, from which he had never returned. It was next affirmed, that a tradesman, passing the church-yard about twelve at midnight, had seen four men carry a dead corpse into that cemetery.

These three facts being joined together, seemed perfectly to agree, and to confirm one another; and all believed some horrible murder had been committed. The relations of the gentleman thought they were called upon to make inquiry into the truth of these allegations: they accordingly came first to the church-yard, where, in company with the sexton, they examined all the graves with great care, in order to discover whether any of them had lately been dug, or had the appearance of containing more than one coffin. But this search was to no purpose, for no alteration had been made upon the graves. It was next reported, that the murdered man had been buried in a plantation about a mile distant from the village. As the alarm was now very general, a number of the inhabitants proposed, of their own accord, to explore it. They accordingly spread themselves over the wood, and searched it with care; but no grave, or new-dug earth, was found.

The matter did not rest here. The person who was said to have seen four men carry a dead corpse into the church-yard at midnight, was summoned to appear before a meeting of the justices of the peace. Upon examination, he denied any knowledge of the affair; but referred the court to another person, from whom he had received his information. This person was examined, and the result was the same as the former. In short, one person had heard it from another, who had received it from a third, who had heard it from a fourth; but it had received a little embellishment from every person who repeated it: it turned out to be the same with Smollett's story of the three black crows, which somebody was said to have vomited.

Upon inquiry at the inn, where it was said the West-India gentleman had lodged, no such gentleman had been seen there; and it was found afterwards, he had never left the West Indies.

Still, however, the veracity of the widow was not disputed; and some dark and secret transaction was suspected. But the whole affair was at length explained, by discovering that she was somewhat deranged by melancholy; and the cries which she at first imagined she had heard, were afterwards imitated by some roguish person, who was highly amused with spreading terror among the credulous.

THE
BENIGHTED TRAVELLER,
AND
HAUNTED ROOM.

A gentleman was benighted, while travelling alone, in a remote part of the highlands of Scotland, and was compelled to ask shelter for the evening at a small lonely hut. When he was conducted to his bed-room, the landlady observed, with mysterious reluctance, that he would find the window very insecure. On examination, part of the wall appeared to have been broken down, to enlarge the opening.

After some inquiry, he was told, that a pedlar, who had lodged in the room a short time before, had committed suicide, and was found hanging behind the door in the morning. According to the superstition of the country, it was deemed improper to remove the body through the door of the house; and to convey it through the window was impossible, without removing part of the wall. Some hints were dropped, that the room had been subsequently haunted by the poor man's spirit.

The gentleman laid his arms, properly prepared against intrusion of any kind, by the bed-side, and retired to rest, not without some degree of apprehension. He was visited, in a dream, by a frightful apparition; and, awaking in agony, found himself sitting up in bed, with a pistol grasped in his right hand. On casting a fearful glance round the room, he discovered, by the moonlight, a corpse, dressed in a shroud, reared erect against the wall, close by the window. With much difficulty, he summoned up resolution to approach the dismal object, the features of which, and the minutest parts of its funereal apparel, he perceived distinctly: he passed one hand over it, felt nothing, and staggered back to the bed. After a long interval, and much reasoning with himself, he renewed his investigation, and at length discovered that the object of his terror was produced by the moonbeams forming a long bright image through the broken window, on which his fancy, impressed by his dream, had pictured, with mischievous accuracy, the lineaments of a body prepared for interment. Powerful associations of terror, in this instance, had excited the recollected images with uncommon force and effect.

THE
HAUNTED BEACH,
OR
POWER OF CONSCIENCE
ON A MURDERER.

BY MRS. ROBINSON.

Upon a lonely desert beach,
Where the white foam was scatter'd,
A little shed uprear'd its head,
Though lofty barks were shatter'd.
The sea-weeds gath'ring near the door,
A sombre path display'd;
And, all around, the deaf'ning roar
Re-echo'd on the chalky shore,
By the green billows made.

Above, a jutting cliff was seen,
Where sea-birds hover'd craving;
And, all around, the craggs were bound
With weeds—for ever waving.[173]
And, here and there, a cavern wide
Its shad'wy jaws display'd;
And near the sands, at ebb of tide,
A shiver'd mast was seen to ride,
Where the green billows stray'd.

And often, while the moaning wind
Stole o'er the summer ocean,
The moonlight scene was all serene,
The waters scarce in motion;
Then, while the smoothly slanting sand
The tall cliff wrapp'd in shade,
The Fisherman beheld a band
Of spectres, gliding hand in hand,
Where the green billows play'd.

And pale their faces were as snow,
And sullenly they wandered;
And to the skies, with hollow eyes,
They look'd, as though they ponder'd.
And sometimes, from their hammock shroud,
They dismal howlings made,
And while the blast blew strong and loud
The clear moon marked the ghastly crowd,
Where the green billows play'd!

And then, above the haunted hut,
The curlews screaming hover'd;[174]
And the low door, with furious roar,
The frothy breakers cover'd.
For in the Fisherman's lone shed,

A murder'd man was laid,
With ten wide gashes in his head;
And deep was made his sandy bed,
Where the green billows play'd.

A shipwreck'd mariner was he,
Doom'd from his home to sever,
Who swore to be, thro' wind and sea,
Firm and undaunted ever;
And when the waves resistless roll'd,
About his arm he made
A packet rich of Spanish gold,
And, like a British sailor bold,
Plung'd where the billows play'd!

The spectre band, his messmates brave,
Sunk in the yawning ocean,
While to the mast he lash'd him fast,
And brav'd the storm's commotion:
The winter moon upon the sand
A silv'ry carpet made,
And mark'd the sailor reach the land,
And mark'd his murd'rer wash his hand,
Where the green billows play'd.

And, since that hour, the Fisherman
Has toil'd and toil'd in vain;
For all the night the moony light
Gleams on the spectred main!
And when the skies are veil'd in gloom,
The murd'rer's liquid way
Bounds o'er the deeply yawning tomb,
And flashing fires the sands illume,
Where the green billows play!

Full thirty years his task has been,
Day after day, more weary;
For Heav'n design'd his guilty mind
Should dwell on prospects dreary.
Bound by a strong and mystic chain,
He has not pow'r to stray;
But, destin'd mis'ry to sustain,
He wastes, in solitude and pain,
A loathsome life away.

THE
SUBTERRANEAN TRAVELLER;
OR
GHOST AND NO GHOST.

The following record is copied verbatim from an old newspaper—*The Weekly Journal, or British Gazetteer.*

"*Bedlam, January* 18, 1719.

"It is not long since one of the female inhabitants of these frantic territories gave the following occasion for a very pleasing entertainment. Some bricklayers happened to be at work here, to repair and clean the passage leading to the common sewer; who going to dinner, and leaving the ladder which descended to it, standing, the said unfortunate inhabitant had a sort of an odd notion, that the workmen had been prying into the secrets of the lower world, and therefore (nobody seeing her) she went down the ladder which led into the common sewer; and, in that subterraneous cavern, finding none to control or stop her passage, she travelled, with great pleasure and curiosity, till she came to *Tokenhouse Yard*, which is near half a mile. There it happened that a couple of young females, coming to the vault, heard a noise below, crying, '*Who the plague are ye? What d'ye make that noise for? What, is the devil in ye?*' Upon which, away flew the women, not staying to look behind them; and coming half-frightened into the house, said, the devil was in the vault. Accordingly, more company going, they still heard the same noise. Upon which they called out, and asked, '*Who's there? What are ye?*' '*The Devil,*' replied the traveller below. '*How came you there?*' said they. '*Nay, how the devil know I?*' answered the mad-woman. '*Why don't you bring me a candle, that I may find my way?*' Finding it certain to be a human voice, they feared somebody might accidentally have fallen in, and therefore they immediately went to work, to deliver the poor wretch from her suffocating thraldom, and found her a lamentable spectacle; so that they began to question her how she came there, and where she lived. She answered *that she was going to Hell, but had lost her way; that there were several in her company, who had got thither, and the gate was shut upon them; that she had lost her way, but should overtake them by and by.* These wild expressions made some of them fancy she was a mad-woman; and, after some consideration, they resolved to bring her hither; when she was presently owned, and the people that brought her let us into the story: but her head still runs on her journey, and she talks of little else."

THE MILKMAN
AND
CHURCH-YARD GHOST.

A man much addicted to the heinous sin of drunkenness, in coming home late one winter's night, had to cross Stepney church-yard; where, close to the foot path, a deep grave had been opened the day before. He, being very drunk, staggered into the grave; it was a great mercy he did not break his neck, or any of his limbs; but, as it rained hard all night, and the grave was so deep that he could not got out, he had but an uncomfortable bed. For some hours nobody passed by; till, shortly after the clock had struck four, a milkman, who had been to the cow-house for his milk, came by, and said to himself, "I wonder what o'clock it is." The man in the grave hallooed out, "Just gone four." The milkman seeing nobody, immediately conceived a ghost from one of the graves had answered him, and took to his heels with such rapidity, that when he reached an ale-house he was ready to faint; and, what added to his trouble, in running, he so jumbled his pails as to spill great part of his milk. The people who heard his relation, believed it must have been a ghost that had answered him. The tale went round, and would have been credited, perhaps, till now, had not the drunkard, sitting one day in the very alehouse the milkman had stopped at, on hearing the story repeated, with a hearty laugh acknowledged himself to be the ghost, and that he had much enjoyed the jumbling of the man's pails, as he ran away, and the loss which it occasioned him.

THE
FAKENHAM GHOST.

The lawns were dry in Euston Park;
(Here truth inspires my tale)
The lonely footpath, still and dark,
Led over hill and dale.

Benighted was an ancient dame,
And fearful haste she made
To gain the vale of Fakenham,
And hail its willow shade.

Her footsteps knew no idle stops,
But follow'd faster still;
And echo'd to the darksome copse
That whisper'd on the hill.

Where clam'rous rooks, yet scarcely hush'd,
Bespoke a peopled shade;
And many a wing the foliage brush'd,
And hov'ring circuits made.

The dappled herd of grazing deer,
That sought the shades by day,
Now started from her path with fear,
And gave the stranger way.

Darker it grew; and darker fears
Came o'er her troubled mind;

When, now, a short quick step she hears
Come patting close behind.

She turn'd; it stopt!—nought could she see
Upon the gloomy plain!
But, as she strove the sprite to flee,
She heard the same again.

Now terror seiz'd her quaking frame:
For, where the path was bare,
The trotting ghost kept on the same!
She mutter'd many a pray'r.

Yet once again, amidst her fright
She tried what sight could do;
When through the cheating glooms of night,
A monster stood in view.

Regardless of whate'er she felt,
It follow'd down the plain!
She own'd her sins, and down she knelt,
And said her pray'rs again.

Then on she sped; and hope grew strong,
The white park-gate in view,
Which, pushing hard, so long it swung,
That ghost and all past through.

Loud fell the gate against the post,
Her heart-strings like to crack,
For much she fear'd the grisly ghost
Would leap upon her back.

Still on, pat, pat, the goblin went,
As it had done before;

Her strength and resolution spent,
She fainted at the door.

Out came her husband, much surpris'd,
Out came her daughter dear;
Good-natur'd souls, all unadvis'd
Of what they had to fear.

The candle's gleam pierc'd through the night,
Some short space o'er the green;
And there the little trotting sprite
Distinctly might be seen.

An ass's foal had lost its dam
Within the spacious park,
And, simple as the playful lamb,
Had follow'd in the dark.

No goblin he, nor imp of sin,
No crimes he'd ever known.
They took the shaggy stranger in,
And rear'd him as their own.

His little hoofs would rattle round
Upon the cottage floor;
The matron learn'd to love the sound,
That frighten'd her before.

A favourite the ghost became,
And 'twas his fate to thrive;
And long he liv'd, and spread his fame,
And kept the joke alive.

For many a laugh went through the vale,
And some conviction too;

Each thought some other goblin tale
Perhaps was just as true..

THE
UNFORTUNATE PRIEST,
AND DEAD BODY.

In a province of Prussia, a man being dead, was carried, as is customary, into the church, the evening previous to the day of his interment. It is usual to place the corpse in an open coffin; and a priest, attended only by a boy of the choir, remains all night praying by the side of the dead body, and on the following day the friends of the deceased come to close up the coffin, and inter the corpse. On this occasion, after the evening service had been performed, every one retired from the church: and the priest, with the young chorister, withdrew to supper; but soon returned, and the former commenced the usual prayers. What was his astonishment, when he beheld the dead body rise from the coffin, and advance towards him. Terrified in the extreme, the priest flew to the font; and, conjuring the corpse to return to its proper station, showered holy water on him in abundance. But the obstinate and evil-minded spirit, disregarding the power of holy water, seized the unfortunate priest, threw him to the ground, and soon, by repeated blows, left him extended, without life, on the pavement. Having committed this act of barbarity, he appeared to return quietly to his coffin. On the following morning, the persons who came to prepare for the funeral, found the priest murdered, and the corpse, as before, in the coffin. Nothing could throw any light on this extraordinary event but the testimony of the boy, who had concealed himself on the first movement of the dead body, and who persisted in declaring, that he saw from his hiding-place the priest killed by the corpse. Conjecture, and endeavours to discover the truth, were alike vain, tormenting, and fruitless. Many resources were tried; for it was not every one that submitted themselves to the belief of a dead body rising to kill a priest, and then quietly resigning itself to the place of its consignment. Many years afterwards, a malefactor, condemned to death for various crimes, and brought to the torture, confessed, that having (for some unknown reason) conceived an implacable hatred against the priest in question, he had formed the design of thus avenging himself. Having found means to remain in the church, he seized the moment of the priest's retiring to supper, withdrew the dead body from the coffin, and placed himself in its stead, in the shroud and other appurtenances. After executing the murder of the priest, he returned the corpse to its place, and got unperceived out of the church, when the friends of the deceased came in the morning to attend the funeral.

THE
VIGIL OF SAINT MARK,
OR
FATAL SUPERSTITION.

Rebecca was the fairest maid
That on the Danube's borders play'd;
And many a handsome nobleman
For her in tilt and tourney ran:

While she, in secret, wished to see
What youth her husband was to be.

Rebecca heard the gossips say,
"Alone, from dusk till midnight, stay
Within the church-porch drear and dark,
Upon the Vigil of St. Mark;
And, lovely maiden, you shall see
What youth your husband is to be."

Rebecca, when the night grew dark,
Upon the Vigil of St. Mark,
Observ'd by Paul, a roguish scout,
Who guess'd the task she went about,
Stepp'd to St. Stephen's church to see
What youth her husband was to be.

Rebecca heard the screech-owl cry,
And saw the black-bat round her fly;
She sat till, wild with fear at last,
Her blood grew cold, her pulse beat fast;
And yet, rash maid, she stopp'd to see
What youth her husband was to be.

Rebecca heard the midnight chime
Ring out the yawning peal of time,
When shrouded Paul, unlucky knave!
Rose, like a spectre from the grave,
And cried—"Fair maiden, come with me,
For I your bridegroom am to be."

Rebecca turned her head aside,
Sent forth a horrid shriek—and died;
While Paul confess'd himself in vain
Rebecca never spoke again.

Ah! little, hapless girl, did she
Think Death her bridegroom was to be.

Rebecca, may thy story long
Instruct the giddy and the young!
Fright not, fond youths, the timid fair:
And you, too, gentle maids, beware;
Nor seek, by dreadful arts, to see
What youths your husbands are to be.

THE
FLOATING WONDER,
OR
FEMALE SPECTRE.

The bridge over the river Usk, near Caerleon, in Wales, is formed of wood, and very curiously constructed, the tide rising occasionally to the almost incredible height of fifty or sixty feet. The boards which compose the flooring of this bridge being designedly loose, in order to float with the tide, when it exceeds a certain height, are prevented from escaping only by little pegs at the end of them; which mode of fastening does not afford a very safe footing for the traveller, and some awkward accidents have been known to arise from this cause. The following singular adventure occurred about twenty years since to a female of the neighbourhood, as she was passing it at night.

The heroine in question was a Mrs. Williams, who had been to spend a cheerful evening at a neighbour's house on the eastern side of the river, and was returning home at a decent hour. The night being extremely dark, she had provided herself with a lanthorn and candle, by the assistance of which she found her way to the bridge, and had already passed part of the dangerous structure, when she unfortunately trod on a plank that had by some accident lost the tenons originally fixed to the ends of it, and had slipped from its proper situation; the faithless board yielded to the weight of the good lady, who was rather corpulent, and carried her through the flooring, with her candle and lanthorn, into the river. Fortunately, at the moment of falling, she was standing in such a position, as gave her a seat on the plank similar to that of a horseman on his nag. It may be easily imagined, that Mrs. Williams must have been dreadfully alarmed at this change of situation, as well as the difference of element. Blessed, however, with great presence of mind, and a patient endurance of evil, the good lady was not overwhelmed by her fall, but steadily maintained her seat on the board; taking care, at the same time, to preserve her candle lighted, rightly supposing it would serve as a guide to any one who might be able or willing to assist her. Thus bestriding the plank, our heroine was hurried down the river towards Newport, the bridge of which, she trusted, would stop her progress, or that she might alarm the inhabitants with her cries. In both her hopes, however, she was disappointed: the rapidity of a spring tide sent her through the arch with the velocity of an arrow discharged from a bow, and the good people of the town had long been wrapped in slumber. Thus situated, her prospect became each moment more desperate; her candle was nearly extinguished! and every limb so benumbed with cold, that she had the greatest difficulty in *keeping her saddle*. Already she had reached the mouth of the Usk, and was on the point of encountering the turbulent waves of the British Channel, when the master of a fishing-boat, who was returning from his nightly toils, discovered the gleaming of her taper, and bearing her calls for assistance, though he at first thought her a witch, yet ventured to approach this floating wonder, and happily succeeded in rescuing Mrs. Williams from a watery grave, and bringing her in safety to the shore in his boat.

Thus was the life of a fellow-creature preserved by a poor fisherman's courage, in not being daunted by what he at first conceived a mysterious light proceeding from some sprite or hobgoblin; but, from duly examining into causes, proved himself both a hero and friend.

POOR MARY,
THE MAID OF THE INN.

Who is she, the poor maniac, whose wildly fix'd eyes
Seem a heart overcharg'd to express?
She weeps not, yet often and deeply she sighs;
She never complains, but her silence implies
The composure of settled distress.

No aid, no compassion, the maniac will seek;
Cold and hunger awake not her care:
Through her rags do the winds of the winter blow bleak
On her poor wither'd bosom, half bare; and her cheek
Has the deathly pale hue of despair.

Yet cheerful and happy, nor distant the day,
Poor Mary the maniac has been!
The trav'ller remembers, who journey'd this way,
No damsel so lovely, no damsel so gay,
As Mary the Maid of the Inn.

Her cheerful address fill'd the guests with delight,
As she welcom'd them in with a smile:
Her heart was a stranger to childish affright,
And Mary would walk by the abbey at night,
When the wind whistled down the dark aisle.

She lov'd; and young Richard had settled the day,
And she hoped to be happy for life:
But Richard was idle and worthless; and they
Who knew him would pity poor Mary, and say,
That she was too good for his wife.

'Twas in autumn, and stormy and dark was the night,
And fast were the windows and door;
Two guests sat enjoying the fire that burnt bright,
And, smoking in silence with tranquil delight,
They listen'd to hear the wind roar.

"'Tis pleasant," cried one, "seated by the fire-side,
To hear the wind whistle without."
"A fine night for the abbey!" his comrade replied,
"Methinks, a man's courage would now be well tried,
Who should wander the ruins about.

"I myself, like a school-boy, should tremble to hear
The hoarse ivy shake over my head;
And could fancy I saw, half-persuaded by fear,
Some ugly old abbot's white spirit appear,
For this wind might awaken the dead!"

"I'll wager a dinner," the other one cried,
"That Mary would venture there now."
"Then wager and lose!" with a sneer, he replied,
"I'll warrant she'd fancy a ghost by her side,

And faint if she saw a white cow."

"Will Mary this charge on her courage allow?"
His companion exclaim'd with a smile;
"I shall win, for I know she will venture there now,
And earn a new bonnet by bringing a bough
From the elder that glows in the aisle."

With fearless good humour did Mary comply,
And her way to the abbey she bent;
The night it was dark, and the wind it was high,
And as hollowly howling it swept through the sky,
She shiver'd with cold as she went.

O'er the path so well known still proceeded the maid,
Where the abbey rose dim on the sight.[193]
Through the gate-way she entered, she felt not afraid,
Yet the ruins were lonely and wild, and their shade
Seem'd to deepen the gloom of the night.

All around her was silent, save when the rude blast
Howl'd dismally round the old pile;
Over weed-cover'd fragments still fearless she past,
And arriv'd in the innermost ruin at last,
Where the elder-tree grew in the aisle.

Well pleas'd did she reach it, and quickly drew near,
And hastily gather'd the bough;
When the sound of a voice seem'd to rise on her ear—
She paus'd, and she listen'd all eager to hear,
And her heart panted fearfully now.

The wind blew, the hoarse ivy shook over her head,
She listen'd—nought else could she hear;
The wind ceas'd; her heart sunk in her bosom with dread,

For she heard in the ruins distinctly the tread
Of footsteps approaching her near.

Behind a white column, half breathless with fear,
She crept to conceal herself there:
That instant the moon o'er a dark cloud shone clear,
And she saw in the moon-light two ruffians appear,
And between them a corpse did they bear.

Then Mary could feel her heart-blood curdle cold!
Again the rough wind hurried by—
It blew off the hat of the one,[C] and, behold,
Even close to the foot of poor Mary it roll'd—
She felt, and expected to die.

"Curse the hat!" he exclaims. "Nay, come on, and first hide
The dead body," his comrade replies.
She beheld them in safety pass on by her side,
She seizes the hat, fear her courage supplied,
And fast through the abbey she flies.

She ran with wild speed, she rush'd in at the door,
She gaz'd horribly eager around:
Then her limbs could support their faint burden no more,
And exhausted and breathless she sunk on the floor,
Unable to utter a sound.

Ere yet her cold lips could the story impart,
For a moment the hat met her view—[D]
Her eyes from that object convulsively start,
For, oh! God! what cold horror then thrill'd through her
heart,
When the name of her Richard she knew.

Where the old abbey stands on the common hard by,

His gibbet is now to be seen:
Not far from the road it engages the eye,
The trav'ller beholds it, and thinks, with a sigh,
Of poor Mary, the Maid of the Inn.

SOUTHEY'S POEMS.

FOOTNOTES:

[C]The hat of one of the ruffians.
[D]She knew it to be Richard's hat.

GILES THE SHEPHERD,
AND SPECTRE.

———————

* *

Giles, ere he sleeps, his little flock must tell.
From the fire-side with many a shrug he hies,
Glad if the full-orb'd moon salute his eyes.

* *

And down a narrow lane, well known by day,
With all his speed pursues his sounding way,
In thought still half absorb'd, and chill'd with cold,

When, lo! an object frightful to behold,[196]
A grisly spectre, cloth'd in silver grey,
Around whose feet the waving shadows play,
Stands in his path! He stops, and not a breath
Heaves from his heart, that sinks almost to death.
Loud the owl hallooes o'er his head unseen;
All else is silence, dismally serene:
Some prompt ejaculation, whisper'd low,
Yet bears him up against the threat'ning foe;
And thus poor Giles, though half inclin'd to fly,
Mutters his doubts, and strains his stedfast eye.
"'Tis not my crimes thou com'st here to reprove;
No murders stain my soul, no perjur'd love:
If thou'rt indeed what here thou seem'st to be,
Thy dreadful mission cannot reach to me.
By parents taught still to mistrust mine eyes,
Still to approach each object of surprise,
Lest fancy's formful vision should deceive
In moonlight paths, or glooms of falling eve,
'Tis then's the moment when my mind should try
To scan the motionless deformity;
But oh, the fearful task!—yet well I know
An aged ash, with many a spreading bough,
(Beneath whose leaves I've found a summer's bow'r,
Beneath whose trunk I've weather'd many a show'r)
Stands singly down this solitary way,
But far beyond where now my footsteps stay.
'Tis true, thus far I've come with heedless haste;
No reck'ning kept, no passing objects trac'd:[197]
And can I then have reach'd that very tree?
Or is its rev'rend form assum'd by thee?"
The happy thought alleviates his pain;
He creeps another step; then stops again;
Till slowly as his noiseless feet drew near,
Its perfect lineaments at once appear;

Its crown of shiv'ring ivy whispering peace,
And its white bark that fronts the moon's pale face.
Now, while his blood mounts upward, now he knows
The solid gain that from conviction flows;
And strengthen'd confidence shall hence fulfil
(With conscious innocence, more valued still)
The dreariest task that winter nights can bring,
By church-yard dark, or grove, or fairy ring;
Still buoying up the timid mind of youth,
Till loit'ring reason hoists the scale of truth.
With those blest guardians, Giles his course pursues,
Till numbering his heavy-sided ewes,
Surrounding stilness tranquillize his breast,
And shape the dreams that wait his hours of rest.

BLOOMFIELD'S *Farmer's Boy.*

A
MAN WITH HIS HEAD ON FIRE, AND COVERED WITH BLOOD.

The following singular adventure is related by a military captain.

"I was coming home one night on horseback, from a visit I had been making to a number of the neighbouring villages, where I had quartered my recruits. It happened there had fallen a deal of rain that day, since noon, and during all the evening, which had broken up the roads, and it was raining still with equal violence; but, being forced to join my company next morning, I set out, provided with a lanthorn, having to pass a strait defile between two mountains. I had cleared it, when a gust of wind took off my hat, and carried it so far, that I despaired of getting it again, and therefore gave the matter up. By great good fortune, I had with me my red cloak. I covered my head and shoulders with it, leaving nothing but a little hole to see my way, and breathe through; and, for fear the wind should take a fancy to my cloak, as well as my hat, I passed my right arm round my body to secure it: so that, riding on in this position, you may easily conceive my lanthorn, which I held in my right hand, was under my left shoulder. At the entrance of a village on a hill, I met three travellers, who no sooner saw me than they ran away as fast as possible. For my part, I went on upon the gallop; and when I came into the town, alighted at an inn, where I designed to rest myself a little. Soon after, who should enter, but my three poltroons, as pale as death itself. They told the landlord and his people, trembling as they spoke, that in the road they had encountered a great figure of a man all over blood, whose head was like a flame of fire, and to increase the wonder, placed beneath his shoulder. He was mounted on a dreadful horse, said they, quite black behind, and grey before; which, notwithstanding it was lame, he spurred and whipped right up the mountain with extraordinary swiftness. Here they ended their relation. They had taken care to spread the alarm as they were flying from this wondrous apparition, and the people had come with them to the inn in such a drove, that upwards of an hundred were all squeezed together, opening both their mouths and ears at this tremendous story. To make up in some sort for my dismal journey, I resolved to laugh a little, and be merry at their cost, intending to cure them of such fright, by shewing them their folly in the present instance. With this view, I got upon my horse again, behind the inn, and went round about till I had rode the distance of a mile or thereabouts; when, turning, I disposed of my accoutrements, that is to say, my cloak and lanthorn, as before, and on I came upon a gallop towards the inn. You should have seen the frighted mob of peasants, how they hid their faces at the sight, and got into the passage. There was no one but the host had courage to remain, and keep his eye upon me. I was now before the door, on which I shifted the position of my lanthorn, let my cloak drop down upon my shoulders, and appeared the figure he had seen me by his kitchen fire. It was not without real difficulty, we could bring the simple people who had crowded in for safety from their terror: the three travellers, in particular, as the first impression was still strong within them, they could not credit what they saw. We finished by a hearty laugh at their expence, and by drinking to the man whose head was like a flame of fire, and placed beneath his shoulder."

THE
INNOCENT DEVIL,
OR
AGREEABLE DISAPPOINTMENT.

The following story is extracted from a letter I received, some time since, from a friend, on the subject of apparitions.

"Returning, one evening in the summer, to my apartments, at a short distance from town, I was invited by my landlady, a brisk young widow, to partake of *un petit souper*, as she termed it. The invitation, of course, I accepted; and, after a pleasant repast, the cloth being removed, various conversation ensued, and the terminating subject was ghosts and hobgoblins. After my attention had been greatly excited by many dreadful recitals, I thought I perceived something black glide swiftly by my feet.

My back at that time being towards the door, I instantly turned round; and, perceiving the same to be shut, I fancied my fear to be only a chimæra arising from the subject we had been conversing on. I therefore replenished my glass; and the subject of spectres was again renewed. In the midst of the discourse, when I was all attention to some dreadful tale, I felt something gently brush the bottom of my chair; when, on looking down, I beheld the most hideous black figure imagination can conceive. It was a monster on all fours, with cloven feet, horns on its head, and a long tail trailing after it as it moved along. My terror, I will acknowledge, was so great, that I instantly jumped up as high as the table, and loudly vociferated, 'Lord have mercy upon me! what is it?' My friendly hostess now begged me to sit down and be a little calm, and she would explain to me the cause of my alarm. The figure having again disappeared, the lady of the ceremonies thus addressed me—'I beg your pardon, Sir, for the fright I have thus occasioned you. It is only a little joke I have been playing off, merely to see whether you were proof against supernatural appearances. A friend of mine having been to a masqued ball in a domino, I prepared the stratagem, by making a head-piece to the dress, with horns, false legs, cloven feet, and a tail. I then instructed my servant, who was by agreement to be in the adjoining room, on hearing a certain part of my story, to open the door as softly as possible, and to make her *entré*, in this habiliment. This she attempted before the plot was sufficiently ripe, when you turned round towards the door, and she retreated. The second attempt too effectually succeeded; for which I again ask your pardon, and am extremely sorry, though luckily it has had no bad effect. But I will never, while I live, again be induced to act so foolishly.'—"

THE
SPECTRE OF THE BROKEN.

The following observations on that singular phenomenon called the Spectre of the Broken, in Germany, is related by Monsieur J. L. Jordan, in the following words.

"In the course of my repeated tours through the Harz (mountains in Germany), I ascended the Broken twelve times: but I had the good fortune only twice (both times about Whitsuntide) to see that atmospheric phenomenon called the Spectre of the Broken, which appears to me so worthy of particular attention, as it must, no doubt, be observed on other high mountains, which have a situation favourable for producing it. The first time I was deceived by this extraordinary phenomenon, I had clambered up to the summit of the Broken very early in the morning, in order to wait for the inexpressibly beautiful view of the sun rising in the east. The heavens were already streaked with red; the sun was just appearing above the horizon in full majesty; and the most perfect serenity prevailed throughout the surrounding country; when the other Harz mountains in the south-west, towards the Worm mountains, &c. lying under the Broken, began to be covered by thick clouds. Ascending at that moment the granite rocks called the Tempelskanzel, there appeared before me, though at a great distance, towards the Worm mountains and the Auchtermanshohe, the gigantic figure of a man, as if standing on a large pedestal. But scarcely had I discovered it, when it began to disappear; the clouds sunk down speedily, and expanded; and I saw the phenomenon no more. The second time, however, I saw this spectre somewhat more distinctly, a little below the summit of the Broken, and near the Heinnichshohe, as I was looking at the sun-rising, about four o'clock in the morning. The weather was rather tempestuous; the sky towards the level country was pretty clear; but the Harz mountains had attracted several thick clouds which had been hovering round them, and which, beginning on the Broken, confined the prospect. In these clouds, soon after the rising of the sun, I saw my own shadow, of a monstrous size, move itself, for a couple of seconds, in the clouds; and the phenomenon disappeared. It is impossible to see this phenomenon, except when the sun is at such an altitude as to throw his rays upon the body in an horizontal direction; for if he is higher, the shadow is thrown rather under the body than before it.

"In the month of September, last year, as I was making a tour through the Harz with a very agreeable party, and ascended the Broken, I found an excellent account and explanation of this phenomenon, as seen by M. Haue on the 23d of May 1797, in his diary of an excursion to that mountain; I shall therefore take the liberty of transcribing it.

"'After having been here for the thirtieth time, ' says M. Haue; 'and, besides other objects of my attention, having procured information respecting the above-mentioned atmospheric phenomenon, I was at length so fortunate as to have the pleasure of seeing it; and, perhaps, my description may afford satisfaction to others who visit the Broken through curiosity. The sun rose about four o'clock; and, the atmosphere being quite serene towards the east, his rays could pass without any obstruction over the Heinnichshohe. In the south-west, however, towards the Auchtermaunshohe, a brisk west wind carried before it their transparent vapours, which were not yet condensed into thick heavy clouds. About a quarter past four I went towards the inn, and looked round to see whether the atmosphere would permit me to have a free prospect to the south-west; when I observed, at a very great distance, towards the Auchtermaunshohe, a human figure, of a monstrous size.

A violent gust of wind having almost carried away my hat, I clapped my hand to it by moving my arm towards my head, and the colossal figure did the same. The pleasure which I felt on this discovery can hardly be described; for I had already walked many a weary step in the hope of seeing this shadowy image, without being able to satisfy my curiosity. I immediately made another movement by bending my body, and the colossal figure before me repeated it. I was desirous of doing the same thing once more; but my colossus had vanished. I remained in the same position, waiting to see whether it would return; and, in a few minutes, it again made its appearance in the Auchtermaunshohe. I paid my respects to it a second time, and it did the same to me. I then called the landlord of the Broken; and, having both taken the same position which I had taken alone, we looked towards the Auchtermaunshohe, but saw nothing. We had not, however, stood long, when two such colossal figures were formed over the above eminence, which repeated our compliment, by bending their bodies as we did; after which they vanished. We retained our position, kept our eyes fixed upon the same spot; and, in a little time, the two figures again stood before us, and were joined by a third. Every movement that we made by bending our bodies, these figures imitated; but with this difference, that the phenomenon was sometimes weak and faint, sometimes strong and well-defined. Having thus had an opportunity of discovering the whole secret of this phenomenon, I can give the following information to such of my readers as may be desirous of seeing it themselves. When the rising sun (and, according to analogy, the case will be the same at the setting sun) throws his rays over the Broken upon the body of a man standing opposite to fine light clouds floating around or hovering past him, he needs only fix his eye stedfastly upon them, and in all probability he will see the singular spectacle of his own shadow extending to the length of five or six hundred feet, at the distance of about two miles from him. This is one of the most agreeable phenomena I have ever had an opportunity of remarking on the great observations of Germany.'—"

SIR HUGH ACKLAND.

The following remarkable fact shews the necessity of minutely examining people after death, prior to interment, and of not giving way to ridiculous fears about supernatural appearances.

The late Sir Hugh Ackland, of Devonshire, apparently died of a fever, and was laid out as dead. The nurse, with two of the footmen, sat up with the corpse; and Lady Ackland sent them a bottle of brandy to drink in the night. One of the servants, being an arch rogue, told the other, that his master dearly loved brandy when he was alive; "and, " says he, "I am resolved he shall drink one glass with us now he is dead." The fellow, accordingly, poured out a bumper of brandy, and forced it down his throat. A gurgling immediately ensued, and a violent motion of the neck and upper part of the breast. The other footman and the nurse were so terrified, that they ran down stairs; and the brandy genius, hastening away with rather too much speed, tumbled down stairs head foremost. The noise of the fall, and his cries, alarmed a young gentleman who slept in the house that night; who got up, and went to the room where the corpse lay, and, to his great surprise, saw Sir Hugh sitting upright. He called the servants; Sir Hugh was put into a warm bed, and the physician and apothecary sent for. These gentlemen, in a few weeks, perfectly restored their patient to health, and he lived several years afterwards.

The above story is well known to the Devonshire people; as in most companies Sir Hugh used to tell this strange circumstance, and talk of his resurrection by his brandy footman, to whom (when he really died) he left a handsome annuity.

AN
AGREEABLE EXPLANATION.

A gentleman of undoubted veracity relates the following story.

"When I was a young man, I took up my residence at a lodging-house, which was occupied by several families. On taking possession of my apartments, I agreed with the old lady of the house, who had two children, to accommodate me with a key to the street-door, to prevent unnecessary trouble to the servant or family, as I should very frequently stay out late in the evening. This was agreed to; and, by way of making things more agreeable, I had always a light left burning for me on the staircase, which was opposite to the outer door. This arrangement being made, things continued very comfortable for some months; till, one night, or rather morning, returning and opening the door as usual, I thought I heard a faint scream—I paused for a few seconds. The cry of 'Murder!' now feebly succeeded. I hesitated how to act, when the cry of 'Murder!' was again more loudly vociferated. This very much alarmed me; and, instead of going forward, I instantly re-opened the street-door, and was in the act of calling the watch, when a tall spare figure, at least six feet high, in a complete white dress, and pointed cap, with a candle in its hand, appeared before me. This unexpected encounter completed my astonishment, and I was about to speak, when the phantom (which proved to be my good old landlady) thus addressed me—'I hope, Sir, I have not alarmed you; but, just before you came to the door, I had a most frightful dream. I thought robbers had broken into my house, and, not content with plunder, had murdered my children, and were about to destroy me; when the noise you made on opening the door increased my agony of mind; and, before I was sufficiently sensible, I screamed out *Murder!* as you must have heard.' This explanation having taken place, the poor woman retired, and was for several days after extremely ill; and I was not a little pleased myself at finding what I at first supposed a supernatural encounter thus terminate, without having recourse to a divine exorcist."

THE
SOMERSETSHIRE DEMONIAC.

On the 13th of June 1788, George Lukins, of Yatton, in Somersetshire, was exorcised in the Temple Church at Bristol, and delivered from the possession of seven devils by the efforts of seven clergymen.

Lukins was first attacked by a kind of epileptic fit, when he was going about acting Christmas plays, or mummeries: this he ascribed to a blow given by an invisible hand. He was afterwards seized by fits; during which he declared with a roaring voice that he was the devil, and sung different songs in a variety of keys. The fits always began and ended with a strong agitation of the right hand; he frequently uttered dreadful execrations during the fits: and the whole duration of this disorder was eighteen years.

At length, *viz.* in June 1788, he declared, that he was possessed by seven devils, and could only be freed by the prayers, *in faith*, of seven clergymen. Accordingly, the requisite number was summoned, and the patient sung, swore, laughed, barked, and treated the company with a ludicrous parody on the *Te Deum*. These astonishing symptoms resisted both hymns and prayers, till a *small, faint voice* admonished the ministers to adjure. The spirits, after some murmuring, yielded to the adjuration; and the happy patient returned thanks for his wonderful cure. It is remarkable, that, during this solemn mockery, the fiend swore, by his infernal den, that he would not quit his patient; an oath, I believe, no where to be found but in the Pilgrim's Progress, from whence Lukins probably got it.

Very soon after, the first relation of this story was published, a person well acquainted with Lukins, took the trouble of undeceiving the public, with regard to his pretended disorder, in a plain, sensible, narrative of his conduct. He asserts, that Lukins's first seizure was nothing else than a fit of drunkenness; that he always foretold his fits, and remained sensible during their continuance. That he frequently saw Lukins in his fits; in every one of which, except in singing, he performed not more than most active young people can easily do. That he was detected in an imposture with respect to the clenching of his hands. That after money had been collected for him, he got very suddenly well. That he never had any fits while he was at St. George's Hospital, in London; nor when visitors were excluded from his lodgings by desire of the author of the narrative: and that he was particularly careful never to hurt himself by his exertions during the paroxysm.

Is it for the credit of this philosophical age, that so bungling an imposture should deceive seven clergymen into a public act of exorcism? This would not have passed even on the authors of the *Malleus Maleficarum*; for they required signs of supernatural agency, such as the suspension of the possessed in the air without any visible support, or the use of different languages, unknown to the demoniac in his natural state.

THE MANIAC,
OR
FATAL EFFECTS OF WANTON MISCHIEF.

Some years ago, a very intelligent, handsome, and promising youth, whose names is Henry Pargeter Lewis, the son of a respectable attorney, in the town of Dudley, was placed for a probationary time, previously to an intended apprenticeship, with a surgeon and apothecary of the name of Powell, in the immediate neighbourhood of one of our great public schools. He had not been there long, before one of the scholars, who lodged at the surgeon's, in league with the servant-boy of the house, devised the following stratagem to frighten him. One night, during an absence of the master, the servant-boy concealed himself under the bed of Henry, before the latter retired to rest, and remained there till the hour of midnight; when, on a preconcerted signal of three raps at the chamber door, it suddenly opened, and in stalked the school-boy, habited in a white sheet, with his face horribly disguised, and bearing a lighted candle in his hand; the servant-boy, at the same moment, heaving up the bed under Henry with his back. How long this was acted is not known: it was done long enough, however, completely to dethrone the reason of the unfortunate youth; who, it is supposed, immediately covered himself with the bed-clothes, and so continued till the morning. On his not rising at the usual time, some one of the family went to call him; and, not answering, except by incoherent cries, was discovered in the state just described.

The melancholy tidings of his situation were conveyed to his friends, on his removal to them; the facts having been disclosed, partly by the confession of the servant-boy, and partly by the unfortunate youth himself, during the few lucid intervals which occurred in the course of the first year after his misfortune.

His father and mother were then living, but they are now both dead: and the little property they left to support him is now nearly exhausted, together with a small subscription which was also raised to furnish him with necessaries, and to remunerate a person to take care of him. He is perfectly harmless and gentle, being rather in a state of idiotcy than insanity; seldom betraying any symptoms of violent emotion, except occasionally about midnight (the time of his unhappy disaster), when, full of indescribable terror, he exclaims, "*Oh! they are coming! they are coming!*" All hope of recovery is at an end; more than twenty years having elapsed since the catastrophe happened.

It is sincerely hoped that this pitiable case may prove a warning to inconsiderate youth; by showing them what dreadful effects may follow such wanton acts of mischief.

EXTRAORDINARY DOUBLE DREAM, WITHOUT ANY CORRESPONDING EVENT.

The late Reverend Mr. Joseph Wilkins, a dissenting clergyman, at Weymouth, in Dorsetshire, had the following remarkable dream, which is copied verbatim from a short account of his life.

"One night, soon after I was in bed, I fell asleep, and dreamed I was going to London. I thought it would not be much out of my way to go through Gloucestershire, and call upon my friends there. Accordingly, I set out; but remember nothing that happened by the way, till I came to my father's house, when I went to the fore door and tried to open it, but found it fast; then I went to our back door, which I opened and went in: but finding all the family were in bed, I went across the rooms only, and walked up stairs, entered the room where my father and mother were in bed, and as I passed by the side of the bed in which my father lay, I found him asleep, or thought he was so; then I went to the other side, and as I just turned the foot of the bed, I found my mother awake, to whom I said these words, 'Mother, I am going a long journey, and am come to bid you good-bye;' upon which she answered me in a fright—*'O! dear son, thee art dead!'* with which I awoke, and took no notice of it more than a common dream, only it appeared to me very perfect, as sometimes dreams will. But, in a few days after, as soon as a letter could reach me, I received one by the post from my father; upon the receipt of which I was a little surprised, and concluded something extraordinary must have happened, as it was but a little before I had had a letter from my friends, and all were well: but, upon opening it, I was still more surprised; for my father addressed me as though I was dead, desiring me, if alive, or whose ever hands the letter might fall into, to write immediately. But, if the letter found me living, they concluded I should not live long, and gave this as a reason for their fears— That on such a night (naming it), after they were in bed, my father asleep and my mother awake, she heard somebody try to open the fore door, but finding it fast, he went to the back door, which he opened, and came in, and went directly through the room up stairs, and she perfectly knew it to be my step, come to her bed-side, and spoke to her these words, 'Mother, I am going a long journey, and am come to bid you good-bye, ' upon which she answered in a fright, '*O! dear son, thee art dead!*' (which were the very circumstances and words of *my* dream); but she heard nothing more, she saw nothing (neither did I in my dream, as it was all dark). Upon this she awoke my father, and told him what had passed, but he endeavoured to appease her, persuading her it was only a dream; but she insisted on it, it was no dream, for that she was as perfectly awake as ever, and had not had the least inclination to sleep since she had been in bed (from which I am apt to think it was at the *very same instant* with my dream, though the distance between us was about one hundred miles, but of this I cannot speak positively). This affair happened whilst I was at the academy at Ottery, in the county of Devon, and I believe in the year 1754; and at this distance every circumstance is very fresh in my mind. I have since had frequent opportunities of talking over the affair with my mother, and the whole circumstance was as fresh upon her mind as it was upon mine. I have often thought that her sensation as to this matter was stronger than mine; and, what some may think strange, I cannot remember any thing remarkable happened thereon; and that this is only a plain simple narrative of matter of fact."

The above relation must convince credulous people how necessary it is, not to place implicit confidence in dreams, or suffer them to make too great an impression on the mind, as they are most frequently merely the result of our waking thoughts.

REMARKABLE INSTANCES
OF THE
POWER OF VISION.

A shepherd upon one of the mountains in Cumberland, was suddenly enveloped with a thick fog or mist, through which every object appeared so greatly increased in magnitude, that he no longer knew where he was. In this state of confusion he wandered in search of some unknown object, from which he might direct his future steps. Chance, at last, brought this lost shepherd within sight of what he supposed to be a very large mansion, which he did not remember ever to have seen before; but, on his entering this visionary castle, to inquire his way home, he found it inhabited by his own family. It was nothing more than his own cottage. But his organs of sight had so far misled his mental faculties, that some little time elapsed before he could be convinced that he saw real objects. Instances of the same kind of illusion, though not to the same degree, are not unfrequent in those mountainous regions.

From these effects of vision, it is evident that the pupil and the picture of an object within the eye, increase at the same time.

* * * * *

The writer of the above account was passing the Frith of Forth, at Queensferry, near Edinburgh, one morning when it was extremely foggy. Though the water is only two miles broad, the boat did not get within sight of the southern shore till it approached very near it. He then saw, to his great surprise, a large perpendicular rock, where he knew the shore was low and almost flat. As the boat advanced a little nearer, the rock seemed to split perpendicularly into portions, which separated at a little distance from one another. He next saw these perpendicular divisions move; and, upon approaching a little nearer, found it was a number of people, standing on the beach, waiting the arrival of the ferry-boat.

* * * * *

The following extract of a letter, from a gentleman of undoubted veracity, is another curious instance of the property of vision:—

"When I was a young man, I was, like others, fond of sporting, and seldom liked to miss a day, if I could any way go out. From my own house I set out on foot, and pursued my diversion on a foggy day; and, after I had been out some time, the fog or mist increased to so great a degree, that, however familiar the hedges, trees, &c. were to me, I lost myself, insomuch that I did not know whether I was going to or from home. In a field where I then was, I suddenly discovered what I imagined was a well known hedge-row, interspersed with pollard trees, &c. under which I purposed to proceed homewards; but, to my great surprise, upon approaching this appearance, I discovered a row of the plants known by the name of *rag*, and by the vulgar, *canker weed*, growing on a mere balk, dividing ploughed fields: the whole height of both could not exceed three feet, or three feet and a half. It struck me so forcibly that I shall never forget it; this too in a field which I knew as well as any man, could know a field."

THE PHILOSOPHER GASSENDI, AND THE HAUNTED BED-ROOM.

In one of the letters of this celebrated philosopher, he says, that he was consulted by his friend and patron the Count d'Alais, governor of Provence, on a phenomenon that haunted his bed-chamber while he was at Marseilles on some business relative to his office. The Count tells Gassendi, that, for several successive nights, as soon as the candle was taken away, he and his Countess saw a luminous spectre, sometimes of an oval, and sometimes of a triangular form; that it always disappeared when light came into the room; that he had often struck at it, but could discover nothing solid. Gassendi, as a natural philosopher, endeavoured to account for it; sometimes attributing it to some defect of vision, or to some dampness of the room, insinuating that perhaps it might be sent from Heaven to him, to give him a warning in due time of something that should happen. The spectre still continued its visits all the time that he staid at Marseilles; and some years afterwards, on their return to Aix, the Countess d'Alais confessed to her husband, that she played him this trick, by means of one of her women placed under the bed with a phial of phosphorus, with an intention to frighten him away from Marseilles, a place in which she very much disliked to live.

THE
GHOST ON SHIP-BOARD.

———————

A gentleman of high respectability in the navy relates the following story.

"When on a voyage to New York, we had not been four days at sea, before an occurrence of a very singular nature broke in upon our quiet. *It was a ghost!* One night, when all was still and dark, and the ship rolling at sea before the wind, a man sprung suddenly upon deck in his shirt, his hair erect, his eyes starting from their sockets, and loudly vociferating he had seen a ghost. After his horror had a little subsided, we asked him what he had seen?—he said, the figure of a woman dressed in white, with eyes of flaming fire; that she came to his hammock, and stared him in the face. This we treated as an idle dream, and sent the frantic fellow to his bed. The story became the subject of every one; and the succeeding night produced half a dozen more terrified men to corroborate what had happened the first, and all agreed in the same story, that it was a woman. This rumour daily increasing, at length came to the ears of the captain and officers, who were all equally solicitous to discover the true cause of this terrific report. I placed myself night by night beneath the hammocks to watch its appearance, but all in vain; yet still the appearance was nightly, as usual, and the horrors and fears of the people rather daily increased than diminished. A phantom of this sort rather amused than perplexed my mind; and when I had given over every idea of discovering the cause of this strange circumstance, and the thing began to wear away, I was surprised, one very dark night, as seated under the boats, with a stately figure in white stalking along the deck! The singularity of the event struck my mind that this must be the very identical ghost which had of late so much disturbed the ship's company. I therefore instantly dropped down from the place I was in, to the deck on which it appeared, when it passed me immediately very quickly, turned round, and marched directly forwards. I followed it closely, through the gallery, and out at the head-doors, when the figure instantly disappeared, which very much astonished me. I then leaped upon the forecastle, and asked of the people who were walking there, if such a figure had passed them? They replied, No, with some emotion and pleasure, as I had ever ridiculed all their reports on this subject. However, this night-scene between me and the ghost became the theme of the ensuing day. Nothing particular transpired till twelve o'clock, when, as the people were pricking at the tub for their beef, it was discovered Jack Sutton was missing. The ship's company was directly mustered, and Jack was no where to be found. I then inquired of his messmates the character of the man; and, after a number of interrogatories, one of them said, that poor Sutton used to tell him a number of comical jokes about his walking in his sleep. Now the mystery was unravelled; and this terrific ghost, which had so much alarmed all the sailors, now proved to be the poor unfortunate Jack Sutton, who had walked overboard in his dream."

The first fellow who spread this report, and who shewed such signs of horror, was found on inquiry to be a most flagitious villain, who had murdered a woman, who he believed always haunted him, and the appearance of this sleepwalker confirmed in his mind the ghost of the murdered fair one; for, in such cases, conscience is a busy monitor, and ever active to its own pain and disturbance.

A REMARKABLE STORY
OF A GHOST,

Thrice called for, as an Evidence, in a Court of Justice.

A farmer, on his return from the market at Southam, in the county of Warwick, was murdered. A man went the next morning to his house, and inquired of the mistress, if her husband came home the evening before; she replied, No, and that she was under the utmost anxiety and terror on that account. "Your terror, " added he, "cannot equal mine; for, last night, as I lay in bed quite awake, the apparition of your husband appeared to me, shewed me several ghastly stabs in his body; told me that he had been murdered by such a person (naming the man), and his body thrown into such a marl-pit, which he then particularly described. The alarm was given, the pit searched, the body found, and the wounds answered the description given of them. The man whom the ghost had accused was apprehended, and committed, on a violent suspicion of murder. His trial came on at Warwick, before the Lord Chief Justice Raymond; when the jury would have convicted, as rashly as the magistrate had committed him, had not the judge checked them. He addressed himself to them in words to this purpose— "I think, Gentlemen, you seem inclined to lay more stress on the evidence of an apparition than it will bear. I cannot say that I give much credit to these kind of stories: but, be that as it will, we have no right to follow our own private opinions here. We are now in a court of law, and must determine according to it; and I know of no law now in being, which will admit of the testimony of an apparition: not yet, if it did, doth the ghost appear to give evidence. Crier, " said he, "call the ghost." Which was *thrice* done, to no manner of purpose: it appeared not. "Gentlemen of the Jury, " continued the Judge, "the prisoner at the bar, as you have heard by undeniable witnesses, is a man of the most unblemished character; nor has it appeared in the course of the examination, that there was any manner of quarrel or grudge between him and the party deceased. I do believe him to be perfectly innocent; and, as there is no evidence against him, either positive or circumstantial, he must be acquitted. But, from many circumstances which have arisen during the trial, I do strongly suspect that the gentleman who saw the apparition was himself the murderer: in which case he might easily ascertain the pit, the wounds, &c. without any supernatural assistance; and on suspicion, I shall think myself justified in committing him to close custody, till the matter can be fairly inquired into. This was immediately done, and a warrant granted for searching his house; when such strong proofs of guilt appeared against him, that he confessed the murder: for which he was executed.

THE
LADY OF THE BLACK TOWER.

BY MRS. ROBINSON.

"Watch no more the twinkling stars;
Watch no more the chalky bourne;
Lady, from the holy wars
Never will thy love return!
Cease to watch, and cease to mourn;
Thy lover never will return!

"Watch no more the yellow moon,
Peering o'er the mountain's head;
Rosy day, returning soon,
Will see thy lover pale and dead!
Cease to weep, and cease to mourn:
Thy lover will no more return.

"Lady, in the holy wars,
Fighting for the cross, he died;
Low he lies, and many scars
Mark his cold and mangled side;
In his winding-sheet he lies.
Lady, check those rending sighs.

"Hark! the hollow-sounding gale
Seems to sweep in murmurs by,
Sinking slowly down the vale;
Wherefore, gentle lady, sigh?
Wherefore moan, and wherefore sigh?

Lady, all that live must die.

"Now the stars are fading fast,
Swift their brilliant course are run:
Soon shall dreary night be past,
Soon shall rise the cheering sun!
The sun will rise to gladden thee;
Lady, lady, cheerful be."

So spake a voice; while, sad and lone,
Upon a lofty tow'r reclin'd,
A lady sat: the pale moon shone,
And sweetly blew the summer wind;
Yet still, disconsolate in mind,
The lovely lady sat reclin'd.

The lofty tow'r was ivy-clad;
And round a dreary forest rose;
The midnight bell was tolling sad,
'Twas tolling for a soul's repose.
The lady heard the gates unclose,
And from her seat in terror rose.

The summer moon shone bright and clear;
She saw the castle gates unclose;
And now she saw four monks appear,
Loud chanting for a soul's repose.
Forbear, O lady! look no more:
They pass'd—a livid corpse they bore.

They pass'd, and all was silent now;
The breeze upon the forest slept;
The moon stole o'er the mountain's brow;
Again the lady sigh'd and wept.
She watch'd the holy fathers go

Along the forest path below.

And now the dawn was bright; the dew
Upon the yellow heath was seen;
The clouds were of a rosy hue,
The sunny lustre shone between:
The lady to the chapel ran,
While the slow matin pray'r began.

And then, once more, the fathers grey
She mark'd, employ'd in holy pray'r;
Her heart was full, she could not pray,
For love and fear were masters there!
Ah, lady! thou wilt pray, ere long,
To sleep those lonely aisles among!

And now the matin pray'rs were o'er;
The barefoot monks, of order grey,
Were thronging to the chapel door:
When there the lady stopp'd the way;
"Tell me," she cried, "whose corpse so pale
Last night ye bore along the vale?"

"O lady! question us no more:
No corpse did we bear down the dale."
The lady sunk upon the floor,
Her quiv'ring lip was deathly pale!
The barefoot monks now whisper'd, sad,
"God grant our lady be not mad!"

The monks departing, one by one,
The chapel gates in silence close,
When from the altar steps of stone
The trembling lady feebly goes;
While morning sheds a ruby light,

The painted windows glowing bright.

And now she heard a hollow sound;
It seem'd to come from graves below;
And now again she look'd around,
A voice came murm'ring sad and slow
And now she heard it feebly cry,
"Lady, all that live must die!
"Watch no more from yonder tow'r,
Watch no more the star of day!
Watch no more the dawning hour,
That chases sullen night away!
Cease to watch, and cease to mourn;
Thy lover will no more return!"

She look'd around, and now she view'd,
Clad in a doublet gold and green,
A youthful knight: he frowning stood,
And noble was his mournful mien;
And now he said, with heaving sigh,
"Lady, all that live must die."

She rose to quit the altar's stone,
She cast a look to heav'n, and sigh'd:
When, lo! the youthful knight was gone;
And, scowling by the lady's side,
With sightless skull and bony hand,
She saw a giant spectre stand!

His flowing robe was long and clear,
His ribs were white as drifted snow.
The lady's heart was chill'd with fear;
She rose, but scarce had power to go:
The spectre grinn'd a dreadful smile,
And walk'd beside her down the aisle.

And now he wav'd his ratt'ling hand;
And now they reach'd the chapel door,
And there the spectre took his stand;
While, rising from the marble floor,
A hollow voice was heard to cry,
"Lady, all that live must die.

"Watch no more the evening star!
Watch no more the glimpse of morn!
Never from the holy war,
Lady, will thy love return!
See this bloody cross; and, see,
His bloody scarf he sends to thee!"

And now again the youthful knight
Stood smiling by the lady's side!
His helmet shone with crimson light,
His sword with drops of blood was dy'd:
And now a soft and mournful song
Stole the chapel aisles among.

Now from the spectre's paley cheek
The flesh began to waste away;
The vaulted doors were heard to creak,
And dark became the summer day!
The spectre's eyes were sunk, but he
Seem'd with their sockets still to see;

The second bell is heard to ring:
Four barefoot monks, of orders grey,
Again their holy service sing,
And round their chapel altar pray:
The lady counted o'er and o'er,
And shudder'd while she counted *four!*

"Oh! fathers, who was he, so gay,
That stood beside the chapel door?
Oh! tell me, fathers, tell me, pray,"
The monks replied, "We fathers four:
Lady, *no other* have we seen,
Since in this holy place we've been!"

PART SECOND.

Now the merry bugle-horn
Through the forest sounded far;
When on the lofty tow'r, forlorn,
The lady watch'd the evening star;
The evening star that seemed to be
Rising from the dark'ned sea.

The summer sea was dark and still,
The sky was streak'd with lines of gold,
The mist rose grey above the hill,
And low the clouds of amber roll'd:
The lady on the lofty tow'r
Watch'd the calm and silent hour.

And while she watch'd, she saw advance
A ship, with painted streamers gay:
She saw it on the green wave dance,
And plunge amid the silver spray;
While from the forest's haunts forlorn,
Again she heard the bugle horn.

The sails were full; the breezes rose;
The billows curl'd along the shore;
And now the day began to close—
The bugle horn was heard no more.

But, rising from the wat'ry way
An airy voice was heard to say—

"Watch no more the evening star;
Watch no more the billowy sea;
Lady, from the holy war,
Thy lover hastes to comfort thee:
Lady, lady, cease to mourn;
Soon thy lover will return."

Now she hastens to the bay;
Now the rising storm she hears:
Now the sailors smiling say,
"Lady, lady, check your fears:
Trust us, lady; we will be
Your pilots o'er the stormy sea."

Now the little bark she view'd,
Moor'd beside the flinty steep;
And now, upon the foamy flood,
The tranquil breezes seemed to sleep.
The moon arose; her silver ray
Seem'd on the silent deep to play.

Now music stole across the main:
It was a sweet but mournful tone;
It came a slow and dulcet strain;
It came from where the pale moon shone:
And while it pass'd across the sea,
More soft and soft it seem'd to be.

Now on the deck the lady stands.
The vessel steers across the main;
It steers towards the Holy Land,
Never to return again:

Still the sailors cry, "We'll be
Your pilots o'er the stormy sea."

Now she hears a low voice say,
"Deeper, deeper, deeper still;
Hark! the black'ning billows play;
Hark! the waves the vessel fill:
Lower, lower, down we go;
All is dark and still below."

Now a flash of vivid light
On the rolling deep was seen!
And now the lady saw the knight,
With doublet rich, of gold and green:
From the sockets of his eyes,
A pale and streaming light she spies.

And now his form transparent stood,
Smiling with a ghastly mien:
And now the calm and boundless flood
Was like the emerald, bright and green;
And now 'twas of a troubled hue,
While "Deeper, deeper," sang the crew.

Slow advanced the morning light,
Slow they plough'd the wavy tide;
When, on a cliff of dreadful height,
A castle's lofty tow'r they spied:
The lady heard the sailor-band
Cry, "Lady, this is Holy Land.

"Watch no more the glitt'ring spray;
Watch no more the weedy sand;
Watch no more the star of day;
Lady, this is Holy Land:

This castle's lord shall welcome thee;
Then, lady, lady, cheerful be!"

Now the castle-gates they pass;
Now across the spacious square,
Cover'd high with dewy grass,
Trembling steals the lady fair:
And now the castle's lord was seen,
Clad in a doublet gold and green.

He led her through the Gothic hall,
With bones and skulls encircled round;
"Oh, let not this thy soul appal!"
He cried, "for this is holy ground."
He led her through the chambers lone,
'Mid many a shriek and many a groan.

Now to the banquet-room they came:
Around a table of black stone,
She mark'd a faint and vapoury flame;
Upon the horrid feast it shone—
And there, to close the madd'ning sight,
Unnumber'd spectres met the light.

Their teeth were like the brilliant, bright;
Their eyes were blue as sapphire clear;
Their bones were of a polish'd white;
Gigantic did their ribs appear!
And now the knight the lady led,
And placed her at the table's head!

Just now the lady *woke:*—for she
Had slept upon the lofty tow'r,
And dreams of dreadful phantasie
Had fill'd the lonely moonlight hour:

Her pillow was the turret stone,
And on her breast the pale moon shone.

But now a real voice she hears:
It was her lover's voice; for he,
To calm her bosom's rending fears,
That night had cross'd the stormy sea:
"I come," said he, "from Palestine,
To prove myself, *sweet Lady, thine.*"

www.ingramcontent.com/pod-product-compliance
Lightning Source LLC
Chambersburg PA
CBHW032227080426
42735CB00008B/752